Operational Risk Management in Container Terminals

This book provides an overview of the operation of container terminals and the associated risks with such operations. These risks are often ignored or not properly investigated by both scholars and practitioners.

Operational Risk Management in Container Terminals explores and discusses the decision rationales and the consequences for these operational risk-handling processes, with in-depth investigation on the container terminals in the Asia-Pacific region. The topics covered include the history and development of the container terminals, the operation of the terminals and risk incurred, the risk-management theories and concepts, rationales and consequences of the risk decisions in container terminal operations, common practices and recommendations on terminal operational risk handling.

Eric Su is currently the General Manager – Engineering of Hongkong International Terminals. He holds an EMBA degree and an DBA degree with City University of Hong Kong and is a Fellow of the Hong Kong Institution of Engineers.

Edward Tang is currently the General Manager – Operations of Hongkong International Terminals. Having started his career as a pier supervisor, Mr Tang has more than 35 years' experience in the container terminal industry.

Kin Keung Lai received his PhD at Michigan State University, USA. He is currently the Chair Professor of Management Science at the City University of Hong Kong. He is the founding chairman of the Operational Research Society of Hong Kong and currently the president of the Asia Association on Risk and Crises Management.

Yan Pui Lee received her Master of Art in Transport Policy and Planning from the University of Hong Kong. She is now pursuing a PhD degree at the Department of Management Sciences of the City University of Hong Kong. Her research interests include transport and logistics management.

Routledge advances in risk management
Edited by Kin Keung Lai and Shouyang Wang

Operational Risk Management in Container Terminals

Eric Su, Edward Tang,
Kin Keung Lai
and Yan Pui Lee

Routledge
Taylor & Francis Group

LONDON AND NEW YORK

First published 2016 by Routledge

2 Park Square, Milton Park, Abingdon, Oxfordshire OX14 4RN
711 Third Avenue, New York, NY 10017

Routledge is an imprint of the Taylor & Francis Group, an informa business

First issued in paperback 2018

British Library Cataloguing-in-Publication Data
A catalogue record for this book is available from the British Library

Library of Congress Cataloging-in-Publication Data
Su, Eric.
    Operational risk management in container terminals / Eric Su,
Edward Tang, Kin Keung Lai and Yan Pui Lee.
        pages cm. — (Routledge advances in risk management ; 6)
    1. Containerization.   2. Container terminals—Risk assessment.
3. Risk management.   I. Title.
    TA1225.S82 2015
    387.1′530681—dc23
    2015003728

ISBN: 978-1-138-78274-7 (hbk)
ISBN: 978-1-138-31694-2 (pbk)

Typeset in Galliard
by Apex CoVantage, LLC

Contents

Figures

Tables

Contributors

Eric Su is currently General Manager – Engineering of Hongkong International Terminals. Dr Su has more than 20 years of container terminal experience in both Hong Kong and Mainland China, including Shanghai, Suzhou and Shenzhen.

Dr Su graduated from the University of Hong Kong in the late 1980s. He is a fellow member of the Hong Kong Institution of Engineers, a member of the Institution of Civil Engineers and a member of the Institution of Structural Engineers. He holds an EMBA degree and an DBA degree with City University of Hong Kong and is currently the director of the Business Environment Council of Hong Kong.

Edward Tang is currently the General Manager – Operations of Hongkong International Terminals. Having started his career as a pier supervisor, Mr Tang has more than 35 years' experience in the container terminal industry. Apart from Hong Kong, Mr Tang has been the senior executive for various major container terminals in Mainland China, including Shanghai, Ningbo, Shantou, Xiamen and Shenzhen.

Starting almost entirely from scratch, Mr Tang and his team created HIT's yard planning system and substantially improved the terminal efficiency through streamlining various operations processes. He was also one of the pioneers in setting up the terminal operating systems and establishing the operations procedures for Shanghai port.

Kin Keung Lai received his PhD at Michigan State University, USA. He is currently the Chair Professor of Management Science at the City University of Hong Kong. Prior to his current post, he was a Senior Operational Research Analyst for Cathay Pacific Airways and an area manager on marketing information systems for Union Carbide Eastern. Professor Lai's main areas of research are operations and supply chain management, financial and business risk analysis and modelling using computational intelligence. He has extensively published in international refereed journals on these areas. He is the editor-in-chief of the *International Journal of Logistics and SCM Systems* and *International Journal of Operations Research*. He is the founding chairman of the Hong Kong Operational Research

Society of Hong Kong and currently the president of the Asia Association on Risk and Crises Management.

In 2009, Professor Lai was the recipient of the Joon S. Moon Distinguished International Alumni Award of Michigan State University and also appointed the Chang Jiang Scholar Chair Professor by the Ministry of Education, China. In 2012, he was ranked among the top four academic authors in the area of business intelligence and analytics worldwide by *MIS Quarterly Special Issue*. In 2013, he was selected as a fellow of the Asia Pacific Association of Industrial Engineering and Management Systems. In 2014, he was the recipient of the Civil and Environmental Engineering Distinguished Alumni Award, Michigan State University, USA.

Yan Pui Lee is pursuing her PhD from the Department of Management Sciences in the City University of Hong Kong. Prior to her PhD study, she was an assistant lecturer, during which she was responsible for conducting courses in transport, logistics and supply chain management. She has received extensive training in this field with her undergraduate and graduate study in management science. She also obtained her master's degree in transport policy and planning.

Miss Lee's main research areas are transport, logistics and support chain management in risk contexts and financial and business risk analysis. She has published a number of papers in these contexts, which include the risk responses/decisions rationales in container terminal operation.

Preface

In the last two decades, development of the container port industry in China and in Hong Kong has been remarkable. Hong Kong has ranked among the top three in terms of throughput in the past eleven years until 2012, while there are five to six ports in Mainland China listed among the top ten container ports in the world in the last couple of years. However, there is a gap between risk-management capabilities and their leading role. Accidents in container terminals not only cause disruption in operations that affect the revenue but also increase the insurance premiums, besides lowering the company's reputation and value. Even with such huge impacts and inefficiencies in relation to risk management, there has been little research focusing on this issue, and there is hardly any research that solely investigates the operational risk in container terminals.

To bridge this gap, this book begins with developing a new model named Stakeholder Uniplanar Risk Evaluation (SURE) for container terminal operational risk management. The SURE model is an extension of two well-known ideas: theory of planned behaviour and protection action decision model – and it is used as the tool for risk assessment in the risk-evaluation process. The application of the SURE model is demonstrated to show how the model can help in the decision-support process.

This book is developed into three parts. Part A (Chapters 1 and 2) is a description and introduction of container terminals. Part B (Chapters 3 and 4) focuses on the operations of the container terminals and their associated risks. Finally, the risk-management theories, strategies and recommendations are discussed in Part C (Chapters 5–8).

Chapter 1 starts by providing a detailed description of the container terminal, which is also an introduction of the whole book. It includes the history of containers and the most basic knowledge needed to study the risk issues of container terminals.

Chapter 2 gives readers a clearer picture of container terminal assets by discussing the major tangible elements that can be found in a container terminal. It ranges from the navigation of vessels to the supporting systems inside the terminal.

Chapter 3 outlines the operations within a terminal, for example, the import, export, transshipment, empty box and dangerous goods handling. Gatehouse, yardside and quayside operations are also covered.

Chapter 4 defines risk, which is important to the discussion in the subsequent chapters for risk management in terminal operations. Then specific risks incurred in the terminal are also discussed.

Chapter 5 discusses the risk management concepts and theories, both existing and newly developed ones. It starts off by listing the processes for risk management. Then well-known models for risk evaluation are reviewed. Most importantly, the new model – Stakeholder Uniplanar Risk Evaluation (SURE) model – is introduced.

Chapters 6 and 7 discuss the application of the SURE model in container terminal operations by referencing research carried out recently over the Asia-Pacific region. The findings of the research are adopted for formulating the strategies and insights in operational risk management, which are discussed in Chapter 8 of this book.

It is also acknowledged that the work is partially support by NSFC Research grant no. 71390335.

Eric Su
Hongkong International Terminals, Hong Kong

Edward Tang
Hongkong International Terminals, Hong Kong

Kin Keung Lai
City University of Hong Kong, Hong Kong

Yan Pui Lee
City University of Hong Kong, Hong Kong

Acknowledgements

The authors would like to express their great gratitude to Mr Gerry Yim and Mr Patrick Lam, who allowed them to take photos in Hongkong International Terminals and Yantian International Container Terminals for the use in this book.

1 Container vessel and terminal

1.1 History of containerization

After the end of World War II, economic gaps among countries were wider than they had been before, and there were huge demands on all kinds of resources. This led to the blossoming of international trade and transportation. At that time, most of the manufacturing industries were located in Europe and the United States, and this was one of the main reasons for the large proportion of transportation in these two regions.

Later on, with the surge in demands, manufacturers had to import raw materials such as crude oil, metal ore, rubber and timber from other countries in the Middle East, South America, India and Australia. Marine transportation in these areas started blooming in the 1950s, and double-digit growth per year was not uncommon in those countries in the next thirty to forty years. However, there was an insufficient supply in marine transportation in terms of vessels and ports, and ship chartering became one of the hottest businesses in Wall Street.

Basically, cargoes in marine transport include crude oil, metal ore, timber (logs), rubber, grains, semi-finished goods (steel, cement, timber plank, pulp products, etc.) and finished goods (consumables, electrical appliances, vehicles, food, etc.). In general, they can be classified into two major categories, bulk cargo and break-bulk cargo (also called "general cargo"). Apart from the form of the cargo, the main difference between these two categories of cargo is their price. For example, the price of coal is in general less than US$100 per ton, but the price of electronic products could be more than US$1,000 each. The sensitivity of transportation cost in comparison to the cost of the cargo does vary significantly. Based on this price difference, the development trend of bulk carriers is to increase their size, while general cargo vessels aim for having higher speed.

In the early days of marine transportation, a general cargo vessel would house different kinds of cargo in its different compartments. With the increase in cargo volumes owing to the increase in international business, the vessel operators were able to develop dedicated vessels designed for a particular type of cargo so as to increase the economic benefits. These included oil tanker, ore carrier, bulk carrier, log carrier and so forth. On the other hand, the size of the vessels increased from several thousand to several hundred thousand tons.

Even though large-scale, purpose-built vessels became more common in those days, finished products that were usually classified as break-bulk cargoes still could not be transported in vast amounts, mainly because the carton box (packing of finished cargo) is not strong enough for stacking high, and wooden and/or metal boxes could not be placed on top. This left a lot of space inside the vessel compartment unused (broken space), and the cost of transportation remained high. In general, only two thirds of the vessel's capacity could be utilized for this type of cargo. In the 1970s, the largest vessel for break-bulk cargo was still around 40,000 displacement tonnage only.

Another major issue faced by the transportation of finished products was burglary. Finished products were usually smaller and lighter but high in price. This made items such as electrical appliances, daily consumables, precious goods and so forth the major targets for burglary during transportation starting from the very beginning. During the early 1960s, plenty of electrical appliances exported from Japan and almost none of the vessels departing from Japan could avoid burglary. Apart from being stolen at the port, these finished products might also be stolen during the voyage. Burglary, as a result, was excluded from marine insurance during a certain period of time.

Starting from early 1960s, some general cargo vessels had started the use of "metal box". Precious products were placed inside these (relatively) large-volume metal boxes, which were locked until they were delivered to the destination port and the boxes were opened by the consignee. This greatly reduced the chance of burglary. However, the weight of the loaded metal boxes usually exceeded five tons. This created another challenge to the general cargo vessels, as their derricks did not have as much lifting capacity in those days. In the late 1960s, some vessels and ports modified their equipment such that the lifting capacity increased to 15 tons, and the container industry started to bloom from that period.

1.2 Containers

The use of containers as the transportation means for commercial use does not have a long history, even though the use of boxes similar to modern containers had been used for combined rail- and horse-drawn transport in England as early as 1792 (World Shipping Council, www.worldshipping.org/about-the-industry/history-of-containerization).

The evolution of modern standard-sized containers started with the U.S. government during World War II, which required a speedy and efficient means for transporting military resources. Originally containers were designed as 8-feet (2.44 m) wide and 8-feet (2.44 m) high. Taller containers have been introduced to the market, including 9 feet 6 inches (2.9 m) and others, which are all classified as "high-cube" in the industry. The lengths of the containers are nominally 20 feet (6.1 m) and 40 feet (12.19 m), and this is how the standard unit of the industry – twenty-feet equivalent unit (TEU) – was derived. Lifting holes, also known as corner casting, are installed at all corners of a container, and these are the lifting points for container-handling equipment, as well

Table 1.1 Dimensions and weights of standard containers

		20' container		40' container		40' high-cube container		45' high-cube container	
		Imperial	Metric	Imperial	Metric	Imperial	Metric	Imperial	Metric
External Dimensions	length	19' 10 ½"	6.058 m	40' 0"	12.192 m	40' 0"	12.192 m	45' 0"	13.716 m
	width	8' 0"	2.438 m	8' 0"	2.438 m	8' 0"	2.438 m	8' 0"	2.438 m
	height	8' 6"	2.591 m	8' 6"	2.591 m	9' 6"	2.896 m	9' 6"	2.896 m
Interior Dimensions	length	18' 8 $^{13}/_{16}$"	5.710 m	39' 5 $^{45}/_{64}$"	12.032 m	39' 4"	12.000 m	44' 4"	13.556 m
	width	7' 8 $^{19}/_{32}$"	2.352 m	7' 8 $^{19}/_{32}$"	2.352 m	7' 7"	2.311 m	7' 8 $^{19}/_{32}$"	2.352 m
	height	7' 9 $^{57}/_{64}$"	2.385 m	7' 9 $^{57}/_{64}$"	2.385 m	8' 9"	2.650 m	8' 9 $^{15}/_{16}$"	2.698 m
Door Aperture	width	7' 8 ⅛"	2.343 m	7' 8 ⅛"	2.343 m	7' 6"	2.280 m	7' 8 ⅛"	2.343 m
	height	7' 5 ¾"	2.280 m	7' 5 ¾"	2.280 m	8' 5"	2.560 m	8' 5 $^{49}/_{64}$"	2.585 m
Internal Volume		1,169 ft³	33.1 m³	2,385 ft³	67.5 m³	2,660 ft³	75.3 m³	3,040 ft³	86.1 m³
Maxi. Gross Weight		66,139 lb	30,400 kg	66,139 lb	30,400 kg	68,008 lb	30,848 kg	66,139 lb	30,400 kg
Empty Weight		4,850 lb	2,200 kg	8,380 lb	3,800 kg	8,598 lb	3,900 kg	10,580 lb	4,800 kg
Net Load		61,289 lb	28,200 kg	57,759 lb	26,600 kg	58,598 lb	26,580 kg	55,559 lb	25,600 kg

as the locations for installing twist locks between containers when they are stacked.

In January 1968, the World International Organization for Standardization (ISO) issued the first notice to define a shipping container, including the terminology, dimensions and ratings. In July 1968, ISO issued the second notice regarding the identification markings of a shipping container. In January 1970, ISO suggested standardizing all corner castings on the top and bottom of the container. In October of the same year, the interior dimensions (cargo space) of "general-purpose containers" (GP boxes) was regulated and defined.

Containers at 45 feet, 48 feet and 53 feet are not uncommon in the industry nowadays, especially for lightweight, bulky cargoes. Their lifting holes are not only at the corners of the containers but also at the 40-foot position. This is because most of the container-handling equipment can only handle containers with lifting holes at either 20-foot or 40-foot positions.

In order to store different types of cargoes safely and cost effectively, various types of containers are now available in the market, including:

- Collapsible
- Gas bottle
- Generator
- General-purpose dry van for boxes, high or half height
- High-cube pallet-wide containers
- Reefer containers
- Open-top bulktainers for bulk minerals or heavy machinery
- Open side for loading oversize pallets
- Platform
- Rolling floor for difficult-to-handle cargo
- Tank container for bulk liquids and dangerous goods
- Ventilated containers for organic products requiring ventilation
- Garmentainers for shipping garments on hangers
- Flush-folding flat-rack containers

1.3 Container vessels

The first container vessel was not purposely built but was converted from oil tankers T2 (oil tankers constructed and produced in large quantities in the United States during World War II) back in the 1940s after World War II. In 1951, the first purpose-built container vessel began operating in Denmark, whilst the first container vessel successfully used commercially was the Ideal X (Levinson, 2006 p. 1). The main feature of a container vessel is the vertical guide rails for aligning the containers within its hull. With the use of robust hatch covers, containers are also stacked above the hatch. At present, the largest container vessel in commercial operation has the capacity of 18,000 TEU.

As mentioned in the previous section, a container usually weighs 10 tons or more when it is fully loaded. When the first laden containers were loaded onto a general cargo vessel, that created a big problem – the vessel that was originally designed for uniformly distributed loads (break-bulk cargo) could not withstand the concentrated load at the four corners of the containers. The simplest way to resolve this problem was to locally strengthen the floor of the compartment.

However, there emerged another problem. Containers stored inside a vessel could not be held in position because of rocking and vibration during voyage, and this problem could not be resolved by simply tying the containers by wires. Finally, a specially designed twist-lock stacker was invented so as to lock all four corner castings of a container, and the stackers at the bottom of the lowest container were welded onto the floor of the compartment, which had been strengthened. This patented design is currently still in use by the container vessels.

The next problem faced by the industry was the lifting capacity of the cranes. This problem was relatively easy to solve by installing cranes with sufficient lifting capacity at both ends of the vessel. The first generation of self-sustained container vessels, therefore, gradually replaced the general cargo vessels for transporting break-bulk cargoes. Not only had they basically protected the goods from burglary, but they also reduced the time for loading and unloading. People therefore started to investigate how the efficiency could further be enhanced. Through various work studies, it was found that the most time-consuming processes were accurately positioning one container on top of another when the crane was still swinging and tying the stacked containers. A new design of container vessel therefore emerged, which was to install vertical guide rails inside the compartment. Because of the great improvement in efficiency, this type of self-sustained cellular container vessel dominated the market.

Besides self-sustained cellular container vessels, a few roll-on roll-off (RoRo) container vessels were built and are still being used. These RoRo vessels are equipped with large ramps that can rest on the quay and allow container tractors to go into their compartment for loading and unloading. This type of vessel is suitable for those ports which do not possess container-handling equipment. Since more and more dedicated container berths have become available since the 1980s, RoRo vessels are not as popular nowadays.

Soon after, the economic potential of pure container vessels was recognized by the industry. The key is the high-value general cargoes such as electrical appliances and luxurious apparel that are not price sensitive to the transportation cost. The most effective means to lower the transportation cost is to further shorten the time while using the same amount of resources. If the possibility of reducing time in every single process is continuously reviewed and executed, containers will definitely be the most cost-effective mode of transportation in the world.

In order to have a breakthrough, the industry unanimously acknowledged that substantial changes had to be made. There were four major criteria: lightweight when the vessel is empty, large storage capacity, high speed and short berthing time. To meet these challenges, most of the unnecessary components of the vessel should be removed. This could be achieved by removing the lifting equipment on vessels. A container vessel, therefore, would only possess storage compartment, ballast tank, fuel tank, engine room and the living and working areas of the crew.

When the lifting equipment was removed from the vessels, ports receiving them needed to equip themselves with ship-to-shore cranes.

This revolution, which involved the construction of pure container vessels and the dedicated ship-to-shore cranes for containers, started in the 1970s all over the world. In the 1990s, the development of container vessels was limited not by the technology of ship building but by the length and width allowed by the Panama Canal. At the same time, container vessels started increasing their storage capacity by making use of the space above the hatch cover, but this would raise the center of gravity of the entire vessel. Stability during the voyage therefore became one of the major limitations in determining the storage capacity. To break through the size limitations, some vessels chose not to pass through the Panama Canal, and this started the development of post-Panama vessels and, recently, the ultra-large container vessel (ULCV). Nowadays, the largest vessel is capable of storing 18,000 TEU.

There are different classifications of container vessel in different parts of the world. For China, container vessels are classified into different "generations" as shown in Table 1.2.

Table 1.2 Major dimensions of container vessels

Container Vessel Type	Vessel Capacity		Major Dimensions			
	Dead Weight Tonnage (DWT) (Range, ton)	Container Capacity (TEU)	Length LOA (m)	Width (m)	Full Draft (full load) (m)	Row of Containers on Board
First Generation	10,000 (1,000~12,500)	200 ~ 1,050	141	22.6	8.3	8
Second Generation	20,000 (12,501~27,500)	1,051 ~ 1,900	183	27.6	10.5	10
Third Generation	30,000 (27,501~45,000)	1,901 ~ 3,500	241	32.3	12	12
Fourth Generation	50,000 (45,001~65,000)	3,501 ~ 5,650	293	32.3	13	13
Fifth Generation	70,000 (65,001~85,000)	5,651 ~ 6,630	300	40.3	14	16
Sixth Generation	100,000 (85,001~115,000)	6,631 ~ 9,500	346	45.6	14.5	17
Seventh Generation	150,000 (115,001~175,000)	9,501 ~ 12,500	398	56.4	16.5	22
Eighth[a] Generation	200,000 (175,001~240,000)	12,501 ~ 18,000	400	60	18~ 21	24

Source: Extracted from: Code of Practice for the Design of Seaport Container Terminals, P.R. China

Note (a): Predicted

The larger is the vessel, the lower is the unit cost of transport per container. Owing to the pressure for driving the cost down, shipping companies will tend to keep increasing the size of the vessel such that the unit cost per container can be further reduced. This in turn creates pressure on the (relatively) old terminals, as they have physical limitations in terms of water draft and quay structure capability and so forth in receiving these ULCV.

Nevertheless, the use of ULCV is based on the hub-and-spoke concept in logistics. If container terminals want to maintain their competiveness in the transshipment business, they shall transform themselves by having more superberths for ULCV, while at the same time there shall be a sufficient number of small berths with suitable equipment for handling smaller vessels, such as the barge berths in Hong Kong.

1.4 Container terminals

With the emergence of global trades, a lot of cargoes is transported by using marine containers. This is one of the major factors for the blossoming of the container terminal industry during the last few decades. Container ports with annual throughput exceeding 10 million TEU are not uncommon today (Table 1.3), and more than half of the top 10 container ports are in China.

Table 1.3 World top 50 container ports 2011 to 2013

Rank	Port, Country	Volume (Million TEUs p.a.)		
		2013	*2012*	*2011*
1	Shanghai, China	33.62	32.53	31.74
2	Singapore, Singapore	32.6	31.65	29.94
3	Shenzhen, China	23.28	22.94	22.57
4	Hong Kong, China	22.35	23.12	24.38
5	Busan, South Korea	17.69	17.04	16.18
6	Ningbo-Zhoushan, China	17.33	16.83	14.72
7	Qingdao, China	15.52	14.50	13.02
8	Guangzhou Harbor, China	15.31	14.74	14.42
9	Jebel Ali, Dubai, UAE	13.64	13.30	13.00
10	Tianjin, China	13.01	12.30	11.59
11	Rotterdam, Netherlands	11.62	11.87	11.88
12	Dalian, China	10.86	8.92	6.40
13	Port Kelang, Malaysia	10.35	10.00	9.60
14	Kaohsiung, Taiwan, China	9.94	9.78	9.64

(Continued)

Table 1.3 (Continued)

Rank	Port, Country	Volume (Million TEUs p.a.)		
		2013	2012	2011
15	Hamburg, Germany	9.30	8.89	9.01
16	Antwerp, Belgium	8.59	8.64	8.66
17	Keihin ports, Japan	8.37	7.85	7.64
18	Xiamen, China	8.01	7.20	6.47
19	Los Angeles, United States	7.87	8.08	7.94
20	Tanjung Pelepas, Malaysia	7.63	7.70	7.50
21	Long Beach, United States	6.73	6.05	6.06
22	Tanjung Priok, Jakarta, Indonesia	6.59	6.46	5.65
23	Laem Chabang, Thailand	6.04	5.93	5.73
24	Ho Chi Minh, Vietnam	5.96	5.19	4.53
25	Bremen/Bremerhaven, Germany	5.84	6.13	5.92
26	Lianyungung, China	5.49	5.02	4.85
27	New York-New Jersey, United States	5.47	5.53	5.50
28	Hanshin ports, Japan	5.32	5.00	4.80
29	Yingkou, China	5.30	4.85	4.03
30	Jeddah, Saudi Arabia	4.56	4.74	4.01
31	Algerciras Bay, Spain	4.50	4.11	3.60
32	Valencia, Spain	4.33	4.47	4.33
33	Columbo, Sri Lanka	4.31	4.26	4.26
34	Jawaharlal Nehru, India	4.12	4.26	4.32
35	Sharjah, UAE	4.12	4.00	3.23
36	Manila, Philippines	3.77	3.71	3.46
37	Felixstowe, U.K.	3.74	3.95	3.74
38	Santos, Brazil	3.45	3.17	2.99
39	Ambarli, Turkey	3.38	3.10	2.69
40	Colon, Panama	3.36	3.52	3.37
41	Salalah, Oman	3.34	3.63	3.20
42	Balboa, Panama	3.19	3.30	3.23
43	Port Said East, Egypt	3.12	2.86	3.2
44	Gioia Tauro, Italy	3.09	2.72	2.30
45	Georgia Ports, United States	3.03	2.97	2.94

46	Tanjung Perak, Surabaya, Indonesia	3.02	2.89	2.64
47	Metro Vancouver, Canada	2.83	2.71	2.51
48	Marsaxlokk, Malta	2.75	2.54	–
49	Nagoya, Japan	2.71	2.66	2.62
50	Durban, South Africa	2.63	2.59	2.71

Source: World Shipping Council

1.5 Container terminals in Hong Kong

Starting from a fishery port in the old days, historically Hong Kong was one of the famous cities for trading since the 1950s. The Victoria Harbour of Hong Kong, located between Hong Kong Island and Kowloon Peninsula, provides a natural typhoon shelter for the vessels. In the old days, the marine transportation of Hong Kong concentrated at the western district of Hong Kong Island, and the maximum size of vessel that it could accommodate was only 2,000 to 3,000 tons. Larger vessels had to moor at the floating buoy in the middle of the harbour. Cargoes would be transferred to the shore via smaller vessels. This type of operation is classified as "mid-stream operations" and is still being used in Hong Kong even though the volume is declining.

Larger berthing facilities, such as Kowloon Wharf, were built starting in the 1960s, and so were the dockyards. Owing to the limitations of berthing facilities at that time, container handling in Hong Kong did not start at these berths but at the dockyard. The first container vessel from United State Line (USL) was received by Whampoo Dockyard, where some of the dockyard area had been fenced off for container handling.

In Hong Kong, the first container berth was planned in the 1960s, and the first dedicated container berth was in operation in 1971. At present, there are altogether nine container terminals comprising 24 container berths in Hong Kong, all of them within the Kwai Chung and Tsing Yi area (also named as "Kwai-Tsing Port").

The name of the first container vessel calling at Kwai-Tsing Port is *Tokyo Express*. Today there are more than 500 vessels calling at Kwai-Tsing Port every week, and the container throughput of Kwai-Tsing Port exceeds 17 million TEU per year.

All container ports in Hong Kong are operated by private entities, and the government plays only the administrative role in port operations. Since the opening of Container Terminal No. 9 in 2003, there have been no more container terminals built in Hong Kong, not even at the design stage. Although there are altogether 24 container berths, total quay length of Kwai-Tsing is 7,694 meters only. This is equivalent to 320 m quay length per berth only, which is not even long enough for the berthing of sixth-generation container vessels unless the copeline of the adjacent berth is made use of.

The existing Hong Kong container terminals and their approaching channel have a water draft of 15.5 m (chart datum). The government has implemented a deepening project since 2013, and the water draft will become 17.5 m upon completion.

The planning for the first container terminal was carried out in the 1960s. The location and the area allowed for further expansions of the existing container terminals are not satisfactory according to the current standard. With reference to the official website of the Hong Kong Container Terminal Operators Association (HKCTOA), the desirable yard-to-quay ratio for effective operations of container terminals shall be around "25 hectare of land per 400 m quay". In Hong Kong, this ratio is as low as "14 hectare of land per 400 m quay". This is one of the critical factors limiting the expansion of the container terminal industry in Hong Kong. The government shall take prompt actions in order to maintain the competitive edge of the container terminal industry of Hong Kong.

2 Major tangible elements of a container terminal

For those readers who are not familiar with container terminals, most of them may that it is just a large piece of land with a waterfront and some equipment, and that the business is no more complicated than moving containers in and out. In fact, a container terminal consists of plenty of elements, and in this chapter are the major items.

2.1 Civil structure

(a) Quay structure

Copeline ("quay") is the most valuable asset in a container terminal. Nowadays, more and more container vessels calling at major ports are longer than 340 meters (sixth generation; see Table 1.2). That means that the length of a vessel is virtually equivalent to a 100-storey skyscraper. In order to withstand the loading of these enormous masses during berthing and mooring, the copeline must be built with heavy-duty, robust quay structure.

Apart from the energy and loadings imposed by the vessels, the quay structure shall also be designed to withstand the loadings of ship-to-shore cranes (also named as "quay crane") manoeuvring above. Most of the quay cranes run on a pair of rails, and therefore the quay structure shall be designed so that rail gauge shall be maintained under all circumstances.

Because of the heavy loading involved, there are two common forms of quay structures – gravity structure and piled-deck structure. Other structural forms such as sheetpile structure, though used by some terminals, are not popular today. Gravity structures are usually formed by caissons. Seawall blocks are seldom used due to their low stability against sliding.

Caissons used in quay structure are normally more than 15 meters tall so as to provide sufficient water draft along the copeline. Each caisson weighs more than a few hundred tons. To explain how it works: a caisson is in fact a large tank made of reinforced concrete, with the lower part usually fabricated in a precast yard on land. The semi-completed caisson will then be transported and placed at the designated location. Water and other backfilling materials such as mud, sand or rock will be placed inside the caisson so as to increase its stability. The upper part of a caisson is usually above the water and cast with reinforced concrete on site. Figure 2.1 is a typical cross-section of caisson type quay structure.

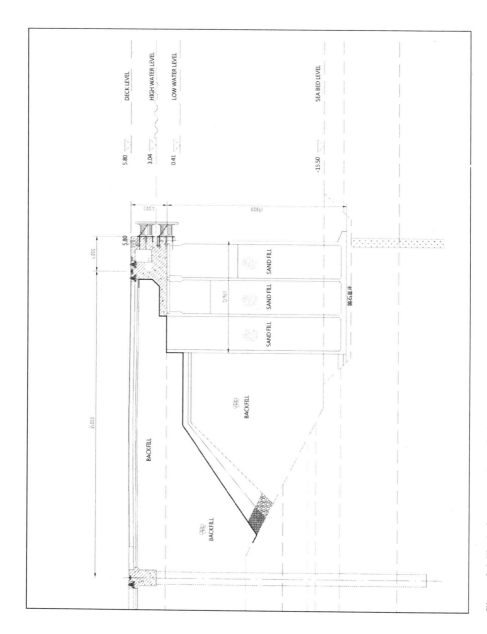

DECK LEVEL

HIGH WATER LEVEL

LOW WATER LEVEL

SEA BED LEVEL

5.80

3.04

0.41

-15.50

5.80

SAND FILL

SAND FILL

SAND FILL

BACKFILL

BACKFILL

BACKFILL

Figure 2.1 Typical cross-section of caisson-type quay structure

The second type of quay structure is the piled-deck structure, and it is the most common form of quay structure in container terminals. Piled-deck structures are usually made with reinforced concrete, and the piles can either be reinforced concrete (with or without pre-stressed) or steel. There is a trade-off in cost and capacity between these two materials. Steel is more expensive than concrete when it is used as marine piles, not only because of the cost of material but also because of the money required for preventing corrosion. However, the loading capacity of a steel pile is usually higher than that of a concrete pile of the same size. Due to its heavy self-weight, concrete piles will not be used in raking piles (raking piles are required for providing horizontal resistance in some situations). Figure 2.2 shows a piled-deck structure under construction.

Splicing of piles was not uncommon in the old days, as there was no suitable equipment for driving long piles. With the availability of large piling barges since the 1980s, piles longer than 50 meters can be driven in one single operation (Figure 2.3). However, only very few contractors possess this kind of piling barge.

Concrete beams and slabs will be cast on top of the piles once they are driven to their designated positions. This casting process is no different from constructing a large-scale industrial building, except that the temporary support and falsework for quay structure are more sophisticated and are suspended over water. If the level of bedrock underneath the quay structure is high, there may be insufficient embedment of pile, and the stability of the structure may be affected, especially when uplift resistance is required for holding the quay crane during typhoons. In this case, a rock anchor and/or rock socket may have to be installed at the pile toe.

Figure 2.2 Piled-deck structure under construction

Figure 2.3 Piling barge

Even though there are numbers of disadvantages of using piles, they are still the most common form of quay structure in container terminals. The main reason for not adopting gravity structures as the preferred structural form of quay is their capability in maintaining the rail gauge. As mentioned, individual caissons are not connected, and the interlocking mechanism is provided through the shear key between them. To cope with the temperature change and thus the possible expansion and contraction, gaps in the expansion joint are required. These joints/gaps may lead to unobservable displacements between caissons, which impose substantial difficulty in maintaining the rail gauge of the quay crane.

Differential settlement between caissons is another major cause of displacement of rails. Quay cranes manoeuvre along the copeline and are not evenly distributed. It is not uncommon that because of the allocation of vessels, these heavy cranes may concentrate operations in a few locations. The frequent application of loadings on a few caissons will accelerate the settlement at those particular locations, and therefore there will be differential settlement and in turn the variance of rail gauge along the quay.

In order to ensure safe and smooth manoeuvring of the heavy quay crane, the rail gauge is critical, and it differentiates the container berths from conventional berths with no ship-to-shore crane. Therefore, although caisson outweighs piled deck in terms of cost, it is not the preferred quay structure in container terminals.

When steel pile is used, the cost for corrosion protection must be taken into account seriously. There are two common means to protect steel piles from corrosion. The first one is to apply corrosion-protection coating to the surface of the piles, while the other means is by filling the steel pile with reinforced concrete. Due to the short lifetime of the coating, reapplication of the coating is required every 5 to 10 years, and it needs to be done underwater. Other measures like cathodic protection can be used as alternatives, but they are often expensive. For the second option, the reinforced concrete inside the pile will take up the loading when the steel pile is corroded. In this case, the steel pile is similar to a sacrificial casing. This option is the most expensive one, but it requires the least maintenance.

Other the other hand, chloride ions that can be found in seawater will penetrate into concrete through the fine cracks and corrode the steel reinforcement inside. This problem does appear on the beams and slabs of deck structures and in caissons. Preventive measures are possible, such as applying a saline coating after removal of formwork or using a formwork liner during concrete casting.

(b) Quay furniture

To ensure the safe and effective operations of a container terminal, four main types of quay furniture need to be installed on the quay structure of container berths. These are fender, bollard, crane rail and power connections.

Fender (Figure 2.4) is the device for absorbing energy during the berthing of the vessels and transforming it to a berthing force that is within the capacity of the quay structure. For small berths, used rubber tyres may be used as the fender, but this is definitely not suitable for container berths.

Figure 2.4 Typical twin-cell fender

For container terminal, each fender unit consists of one to two units of large-diameter rubber tube installed horizontally. Usually steel frame (frontal panel) with resin boards facing the waterside will be used together with the fender unit. The function of this frontal panel is to spread the loading onto the entire fender and to reduce friction between the rubber and the hulls of vessels. Depending on the horizontal curvature of the vessels the berth is going to serve, fender units are usually at 15 to 20 meters apart. Resin panels are installed on the front face of the steel frame in order to reduce the friction between the vessel and the fender.

Bollard is used for tying the mooring ropes (towropes) of a vessel when it is moored. Cast iron is the most common type of material for making the bollard. In general, more bollards provide greater flexibility to berth planning. However, apart from cost, the small clearance between the bollards may limit the operations of roll-on-roll-off (RoRo) vessels, which require the tractor to move into the vessel directly via a ramp between the vessel and the quay. Furthermore, the spacing of bollards must be sufficient for loading and unloading of terminal equipment such as quay cranes. For container terminals, the spacing of bollards is usually 15 to 20 m apart, and the capacity of bollards ranges from 50 to 200 tons (Figure 2.5).

Crane rail (Figure 2.6) is used for guiding the proper manoeuvring of a quay crane. The self-weight of a quay crane is more than 1,000 tons, sometimes even

Figure 2.5 Typical bollard

Figure 2.6 Typical crane rail system for QC

Figure 2.7 Typical HV cable trough

more than 1,500 tons depending on its size. With such heavy load imposed by the quay crane, the crane rail of a quay structure is one of the few largest rails in the world and is a few times larger than conventional train rail in terms of cross-sectional area. Usually there are no joints in this crane rail so as to allow the smooth manoeuvring of the quay crane. As such, a special rail-fixing mechanism, which allows longitudinal movement of the rail due to temperature change, is required to hold the continuous rails in position all the way through. This mechanism usually includes a steel rail clamp with rubber nose in between rail and clamp and a rubber pad underneath the rail that is strong enough to prevent the rail from moving sideways.

A quay crane requires high-voltage (HV) electricity at around 10,000 volts to operate, and thus there shall be proper facilities to provide high-voltage power but at the same time allow the cable to go along with the quay crane when it manoeuvres. To prevent the HV cable from damage, cable trough will be installed, usually on the water side of the waterside crane rail. These cable troughs may be sufficient to embed two to three layers of cables, depending on the number of quay cranes installed and the coverage of the quay cranes.

(c) Stacking yard and landside facilities

A container terminal requires a large piece of land for stacking containers. Since a terminal is built next to a waterfront, the land required for stacking is usually formed by reclamation. As such, ground settlement is always a problem for terminals. However, this is an engineering issue, and therefore it will not be discussed here.

In order to maximize the efficiency of operations, most terminals today use tractors instead of straddle carriers for internal transportation of containers, especially in Asia. In general, a straddle carrier can stack containers up to three high only, and it requires clearance between each stack of containers so as to allow the passage of a straddle carrier.

For tractor mode, containers are stacked by rubber-tyred gantry crane (RTGC) or rail-mounted gantry crane (RMGC) up to six high (or even seven high in some extreme cases). The containers are closely packed to 6 wide (for RTGC) to 12 wide or more (for RMGC). This mode of stacking uses more equipment (tractor plus RTGC/RMGC) than the straddle carrier mode, but it provides substantially higher stacking capacity owing to higher stacking and less space between stacked containers. For terminals at which the price of land is high, tractor mode is the preferred option.

Reefer containers require electrical power supplied by the terminal for maintaining the low temperature inside. As these containers are stacked, terminals in general will equip them with reefer racks such that the yard operators can work in a safe environment, such as the plugging and unplugging of reefer sockets, to monitor the temperature of the reefer containers. Figure 2.8 shows a typical reefer rack at a container terminal.

The gatehouse is the facility for dealing with the external tractors. It mainly consists of traffic lanes and an office (lodge). The quantity of traffic lane is determined by the capacity and the throughput mix (such as the percentage of transshipment) of a terminal. Equipment installed at these lanes (but not necessary for all lanes) includes CCTV, scanner, weighbridge, card reader and so forth. The gatehouse office is the facility for handling the documentation of the containers and assigning the location to which the external tractor will go for grounding or

Figure 2.8 Reefer rack

Figure 2.9 Gatehouse

picking up containers. Further details of the operations of the gatehouse are discussed in Chapter 3.

Cranes used in a container terminal are usually enormous. It is difficult to transport these enormous cranes outside the terminal for repair and maintenance. As a result, almost all terminals will have their own workshop to carry out the repair and maintenance. Heavy components such as spreader, engine, motor and the like will be dismantled from the equipment for repair and maintenance, and therefore overhead bridge cranes will usually be installed inside the workshop.

In order to provide sufficient power for lifting the heavy containers at the quayside, a container terminal has to consume huge amounts of electricity. This

Figure 2.10 Equipment workshop (from outside)

Figure 2.11 Equipment workshop (from inside)

electrical power is transmitted in high voltage (around 10,000 kV) to minimize the power loss during transmission. As such, container terminals will usually have their own electrical substation(s) and electricians to manage the power supply.

To ensure a reliable power supply to the operations, electricity for the container terminal is usually fed from two independent sources (also known as "dual feed"). In case the local power plant of the city cannot provide more than one power source, some container terminals may choose to equip themselves with a massive generator(s) as redundancy.

Figure 2.12 Electrical substation

Figure 2.13 Fuel station

Apart from electrical power, container terminals consume huge amounts of fuel, mainly diesel, for their yard cranes and tractors. For large terminals, fuel trucks may have to work around the clock for filling up the empty tanks of the equipment. Therefore, most of the terminals have equipped themselves with fuel tanks, usually underground, inside their yard. Furthermore, in order to reduce the amount of emissions, a few terminals (such as Yantian Port in Shenzhen, China) are using liquefied natural gas (LNG) for their tractors, and therefore LNG stations have to be built inside the terminal.

2.2 Equipment for container handling

In order to provide efficient service, plenty of equipment is used in a container terminal, and the rest of the chapter introduces the major pieces which are unique to container terminal operations.

(a) Quay crane

"Quay crane" (QC) is jargon used by the industry to describe the ship-to-shore crane for container operations. For inbound cargo, the QC picks up containers from the vessel and loads them onto tractors, and the cycle is just the reverse for outbound cargo.

For QCs, plenty of major parameters are important, such as speed. But for stakeholders in the industry, the most important three major parameters are outreach, lifting height and lifting capacity.

"Outreach" is by definition how far the QC can reach in terms of lifting a container at the farthest end of a container vessel. As the width of container vessels, especially for ULCV, keeps increasing, there is a tendency for container terminals to buy new QCs with sufficient buffers to cover the next or even the next two generations of container vessels. The outreach can be measured in meters. But in the industry, it is more common to measure it by the "number of across". The higher the number of across, the larger the capacity of a vessel. The QC should be able to provide sufficient outreach so as to handle the outermost row of containers. Otherwise, the vessel may have to berth twice, one for the board side and the other for starboard side. For a 24-across vessel, the length of outreach must be around 72 m, measured from the centreline of the seaside crane rail.

Another major parameter for the QC is the lifting height. With the increase in vessel size, there are more containers stacked above the hatch covers. For Triple-E-class container vessels, a maximum of 10 layers of containers can be stacked above the hatch cover. If the container vessel is loaded with empty containers and the water level is high, the containers at the top may hit the QC. As a result, the QC for handling ULCV must have a lifting height of 46 to 49 m, measured from the bottom of the spreader when it is parked at its uppermost position to the top of the seaside crane rail. This dimension is equivalent to the height of a 15-storey building. Operators at the driving cabinet, usually located at the boom level of a QC, need to pick up and drop the containers from this distance, not to mention

Figure 2.14 Quay crane

the additional height when picking a container up from the very bottom of the hull of a vessel.

(b) Yard crane

As the containers and the vessels will not arrive at the terminal at the same time, nor will the tractor for picking up an inbound container arrive at the terminal simultaneously with the vessel, a container yard is needed to serve as a temporary storage buffer for containers.

Containers are stacked up in order to maximize the use of land. Laden containers will be stacked up to seven containers high (in general six high in Hong Kong), subject to the flatness of the land. Empty containers could be stacked up to eight high and are closely packed and tied together by lashing to avoid falling during strong wind.

Rubber-tyred gantry cranes (RTGC; Figure 2.16a) or rail-mounted gantry cranes (RMGC; Figure 2.16b) are often used for stacking the laden containers in the yard. Straddle carriers are used in some of the ports in Europe, but their popularity has decreased because of the limitation in stacking height and capacity. The RMGC operates with electricity, and a cable reel is used as the medium for obtaining electrical power.

In general, the gantry speed of RMGC is higher; its gantry movement is guided by the rail. However, RMGC can only travel within the length of the gantry rail, and the repair and maintenance can only be carried out within the stacking yard. On the other hand, an RTGC is capable of reaching almost every corner of the yard, as its wheels can turn up to 90 degrees, and it can travel to a designated (workshop) area for repair and maintenance.

Figure 2.15a Twin-lift and tandem spreader of quay crane

Figure 2.15b

Figure 2.16a Rubber-tyred gantry crane and rail-mounted gantry crane

Figure 2.16b

(c) Stacker and forklift

A reach stacker (Figure 2.17) can lift and stack laden containers up to six high. It is used in places where RTGC or RMGC cannot reach, for example, in a stacking yard of irregular shape or quay deck. An empty stacker (Figure 2.18) is designated for handling empty containers, and thus the lifting capacity is around 5 tons. It can stack empty containers up to eight high.

Figure 2.17 Reach stacker

Figure 2.18 Empty stacker

Apart from stackers, some manufacturers produce forklifts for laden and for empty containers.

(d) Terminal tractor and chassis

Terminal tractors (Figure 2.19) and chassis (Figure 2.20) are used for transporting containers between quay front and stacking yard. Unlike the tractor and chassis used on public roads, a terminal tractor will not travel at high speed within the terminal area, and therefore it has no corner lock on the chassis. Instead, guide plates will be installed on all perimeters of the terminal chassis, which prevent the container from falling. This saves time for the locking and unlocking of the containers.

Figure 2.19 Terminal tractor

Figure 2.20 Internal chassis

2.3 Terminal operation system

Modernized container terminals rely heavily on advanced terminal operation systems (TOS) to maintain their high efficiency. A TOS is basically divided into two sub-systems, including vessel operation system (VOS) and yard operation system (YOS).

VOS mainly focuses on how the containers are placed on a vessel. For example, when a vessel has to call at three ports before it arrives at its destination, and there are containers loading and unloading in all three ports, the most critical issue is to avoid placing the containers to be unloaded at the third port of call on top of those for the second port of call. Otherwise, there will be plenty of shuffling actions at the second port of call. If the number of port calls is more than six and the containers to be loaded and unloaded exceed 1,000 (which is very common in the industry), the situation will become very complicated and inefficient.

Another consideration is the ship stability. In general, the maximum water draft of a container vessel is less than 15 m, but the maximum height of a vessel could be more than 50 m, measured from the water surface. In that case, there will be high risk of toppling if the heavy containers are placed on top while the light-weight containers are placed at the bottom. Therefore, the VOS shall also take into account the sequence of placing containers as well as the ship stability.

Once the stowage plan is determined, VOS will, depending on the number of quay cranes deployed and the number of containers to be handled, determine the best mix of resources, including yard cranes, tractors, gangs and so forth, for loading and unloading containers of that particular vessel. The sequence of loading and unloading is also critical, as there could be chances of trimming, tilting, hogging and sagging of the vessel if the containers are concentrated at certain locations.

Taking into account the factors mentioned and other associated elements, the VOS will then provide real-time operational information for terminal operators to determine the berthing schedule of the port. The appropriateness of the berthing schedule will basically determine the overall efficiency of the terminal.

Similar to the VOS, the YOS is also a complicated planning process. Although there do not exist stability issue as mentioned for vessels, there are various categories of containers being stored and stacked in the container yard, including shipping company, inbound, outbound, transshipment, empty, date of vessel call, size of container and so on. Any minor overlooking of the details affects not only the vessel concerned but also the overall efficiency of the terminal. Worse still, it may affect the traffic in the vicinity of the terminal.

This enormous container-stacking plan has to be based on an overall "grounding strategy". The computer system will, based on this strategy and other factors and considerations, determine the exact location at which each container shall be placed.

3 How a container terminal operates

3.1 Container shipping

Based on the agreements between the shipper and the shipping company, container shipping can be broadly be classified into four categories.

(a) Full container load shipping

Full container load shipping means a shipper enters into an agreement with a shipping company to consign an entire container of goods, or a shipper arranges the container himself without renting from a shipping company. Usually the shipper will make the full use of the volume or the loading capacity of a container and put as much cargo as possible into a container.

A shipper declares the information of the export cargoes by completing a manifest through the shipping company or a shipping agent and collects an empty container from a designated depot. The empty container will then be transported to the location of the cargoes, and the shipper will arrange for the loading of cargoes into the container. Once the loading process is completed, the door of the container will be locked by the shipper by using a "container seal", and the container will then be delivered to the designated terminal via its entry gate (gate-in). The container terminal will place the container in its yard for temporary storage until the target vessel arrives. By then, the container terminal will arrange its internal tractor to transport the container to the quayside for loading onto the vessel. As such, the export process is complete.

Through the voyage at sea, the target arrives at the destination port (arrival port). By that time, the import process begins. The arrival port will arrange the unloading of the container from the target vessel and store the container in its yard until the consignee arranges a tractor to collect it. Using the shipping order sent by the shipper, the consignee will convert it to a delivery order (bill of lading) from the local shipping company (shipping company at the destination port). With the proper delivery order, the consignee will be able to arrange the collection of the container at the arrival port.

(b) Less container load shipping

Less container load shipping means the shipper's cargoes cannot make full use of the capacity of a container, and the shipper shares part of the container capacity with other shippers, usually to the same destination port. Once the shipper consigns a shipping company for this type of transportation, the (break-bulk) cargoes will be delivered to a container freight station (CFS) or a third-party logistics (3PL) company. The CFS or 3PL will consolidate the cargoes from different shippers into a container and complete with a seal. Then the CFS or 3PL will arrange the delivery of the container to the designated terminal for export. The processes thereafter are more or less the same as those mentioned earlier except that once the container arrives at the destination port, the CFS or 3PL will deliver the container to its warehouse or logistics center for unloading. Instead of transporting the entire container from the terminal to the consignee directly, different consignees will collect the respective (break-bulk) cargoes at the warehouse or logistics center.

(c) Transshipment

As can be understood from the name itself, transshipment means the container cannot be transported from the departure port to the destination port by using one vessel only. The vessel that collects the container at the departure port is named as "first carrier". When it arrives at a transshipment port, the container will be off-loaded to the yard for temporary storage until another target vessel ("second carrier") arrives and collects it. For a transshipment port, the process for unloading a transshipment container is called "transshipment in", while that for loading it to another vessel is called "transshipment out".

(d) Empty re-positioning

All shipping companies will have their containers for the use of the shipper, either owned by themselves or leased from external parties. In general, these container leasing companies will not be involved in the consigning business but focus on providing the leasing service.

Shipping companies have to maintain a sufficient quantity of empty containers in different ports so as to provide their service. As a result, they will have depots, either owned by themselves or leased from others, for storing these empty containers. In order to improve the utilization of the empty containers, the management of empty containers, such as the quantities, the sizes and the types to be stored, is very crucial to a shipping company.

3.2 Operation flow

The operational flow of a container terminal can be briefly described as: (i) obtaining the information from shipping companies, including the date/time of arrival, details of the container to be loaded and unloaded and so on; (ii) planning of vessel arrival and departure date/time based on the availability of berth and yard; (iii) real-time management of the terminal operations; and (iv) data reporting and analysis of the information obtained from actual operations.

The movement of containers inside a terminal can be briefly divided into three major modes. This classification is based on the documentation provided to the terminal operator from the shipping company or other related entities. For example, the official document provided by a shipping company indicates that the container is transported from Port A to Port B by sea, and the consignee will collect the container (and cargo) at Port B. As such, the container at Port A is considered "export", while at Port B it is considered "import". In many cases, the container may transit from one vessel to another vessel at Port C before arriving at Port B; the container at Port C is then considered "transshipment".

However, the container may have been transported through other means prior to arriving at Port A, or the container may be transported to another destination after the consignee at Port B has collected the container. The process that happens before or after the voyage of the container from Port A to Port B will not be taken into account in the terminal operation process if it is not reported to Ports A and B. As a result, this classification of container movement is with respect to an individual container terminal and not the entire logistic chain.

(a) Inbound container (I/B)

For inbound, the container is discharged from vessel to shore and is transported to the yard area by terminal equipment for temporary storage. The consignee will assign an external tractor to collect the container in the terminal and deliver it to the recipient. After the cargoes are taken out by the recipient, the empty container will be returned to the terminal or the designated empty depot assigned by the shipping company.

The detailed operation flow of an inbound container (after the vessel has berthed and agreed on the loading/unloading plan with the terminal operator) is as follows:

- quayside terminal stevedores unlash the container on board
- quay crane discharges the laden inbound containers from ship to quayside
- load the container onto internal tractor
- quayside stevedores remove the twistlock at the bottom of the container
- internal tractor transports the container to stacking yard
- yard crane places the container into the designated position

By then, the container will be stored in the stacking yard and wait for the consignee to collect it. When the designated external tractor of the consignee arrives at the terminal, the following process continues:

- consignee tractor (bare chassis) gate-in and clearing all documentation required

- proceed to assigned yard location
- yard crane loads the container to consignee tractor
- tractor driver locks the container with chassis pins
- container inspector inspects the container integrity
- documentation clearance at out-gate
- transport the container to consignee assigned location
- devanning the container at consignee premise
- consignee returns the empty container to the terminal (or assigned off-dock empty depot)

(b) Outbound container (O/B)

For outbound, the container is delivered by external tractor to the terminal for temporary storage. It will be transported to the quayside by terminal equipment when the designated vessel arrives and will be loaded onto the vessel.

The detailed operation flow of an outbound container is as follows:

- shipper arranges the collection of empty container from terminal (or from assigned off-dock empty depot) and transports it to the location where the cargoes are to be transported
- shipper places cargoes in empty container, sealing container door and proceeding to terminal
- shipper tractor carrying the laden container arrives at terminal
- container inspector inspects the container integrity
- documentation clearance at in-gate and proceed to the assigned yard location
- tractor driver unlocks the chassis pins
- yard crane picks up the container for storage in container yard
- shipper tractor leaves the terminal with empty chassis

By then, the container will be stored in the stacking yard and wait for the arrival of its designed vessel. When the vessel arrives, the following process continues:

- terminal operator assigns internal tractor to collect the container
- yard crane picks up the container and loads it onto the internal tractor
- internal tractor proceeds to the quayside of designated berth
- quayside stevedores install twistlock to the bottom of the container
- quay crane loads the container on board the vessel to its designated position
- quayside stevedores complete the lashing of the containers on the vessel
- vessel departs the terminal

(c) Transshipment (T/S)

For transshipment, the container is discharged from vessel (also named as the "first carrier") to shore and is transported to the yard area by terminal equipment for temporary storage. It will be re-transported to the quayside by terminal equipment when the target vessel (also named the "second carrier") arrives and will be loaded onto the target vessel.

A detailed operation flow of a transshipment container is as follows:

- first carrier arrives at the terminal and berths alongside
- quayside stevedores of the terminal unlash the container on board
- quay crane discharges the laden inbound containers from ship to quayside
- load the container onto internal tractor
- quayside stevedores remove the twistlock at the bottom of the container
- internal tractor transports the container to stacking yard
- yard crane places the container in the designated position

By then, the container will be stored in the stacking yard and wait for the arrival of the second carrier. When the second carrier berths at the terminal, the following process continues:

- terminal operator assigns internal tractor to collect the container
- yard crane picks up the container and loads it onto the internal tractor
- internal tractor proceeds to the quayside of designated berth
- quayside stevedores install twistlock to the bottom of the container
- quay crane loads the container on board the vessel to its designated position
- quayside stevedores complete the lashing of the containers on the vessel
- second carrier departs the terminal

As described, an inbound container will generate three tractor trips to the terminal (quayside to yard, yard to external and empty return), and so will an outbound container. A transshipment container will generate two trips instead of three. As a result, a natural container move of the terminal will generate 2.5 to 3 tractor trips, depending on the throughput mix. For a terminal with annual throughout of 5 million TEU (which is only one third of the Kwai-Tsing Port), the natural container moves will number around 3.5 million, and the number of tractor trips will be close to 10 million per year. That means there will be around 25,000 to 30,000 trips per day! Traffic design and traffic management are critical in preventing traffic jams and accidents within the terminal.

3.3 Quayside operations

Quayside operation is a crucial part of a container terminal, and it includes the following sub-categories:

- **Vessel berthing and departure** – Except for the small barges or vessels of less than certain gross tonnage, most of the container vessels require mandatory pilotage service from the local pilot authority when entering and leaving the port area. The pilot will be on board at a designated pilot boarding station, and the whole navigation within the port region will be under pilot supervision. The pilot will also communicate with the terminal pier supervisor via radio during the berthing process.

- **Lashing on vessel** – In order to ensure the containers stacked above hatch covers of the vessels do not fall off during the voyage, these containers will be tied together; this activity is known as "lashing". There are typical lashing patterns for different container stacking arrangements, and usually they are diagonal. Specific equipment will be used to help stevedores to reach containers stacked more than two high.
- **Signalling and checkers** – During the loading and unloading of the containers, there shall be one on-board "signal-man" and one pier-side checker working together, one on board the vessel and the other on the quayside. They will use wireless handheld radios and hand signals to communicate with the quay crane operator.
- **Vessel movement** – Even when the vessel is moored at the berth, various factors will affect the rise and fall of the vessel, such as the tide and the loading/unloading of the containers. As such, the quayside supervisor shall communicate with the vessel crew and ensure the mooring ropes are not loosened or broken.
- **Traffic control** – Traffic flow at quayside is mainly determined by how the vessel is berthed. Generally speaking, the most cost-efficient and safe traffic flow direction along quayside is from stern to bow. There are usually four to six traffic lanes under the quay cranes, and each quay crane will utilize one traffic lane for safe traffic management. Moreover, the traffic lanes along the quayside are not permanent, as some of them may be occupied by stacked containers and hatch covers, especially for the traffic lanes at the backreach area.

3.4 Yard operations

The container yard is the place for storing laden and empty containers. The success of the yard operations depends on how fast a container can be retrieved and picked up when required, especially for the ones that are stored at the very bottom of a stack.

A reefer container is one of the laden containers, and it requires the special attention of yard operations to maintain the temperature inside the container. This includes the provision of electricity and the monitoring of temperature at regular intervals.

Since the traffic on the quayside and in the container yard does not allow reverse flow, sometimes a container has to be turned 180 degrees horizontally before it is transported to the quayside. In that case, the doors of the containers will face the same direction when they are on board, and this facilitates the unloading process when the containers arrive at the destination port.

Unlike the traffic flow at quayside, which involves mainly the internal tractors, traffic flow in the container yard is complicated, as it involves the manoeuvring of internal tractors, external tractors and yard cranes. External tractors are not owned by the container terminal, and therefore it will be difficult to enforce any regulation, as the yard itself is not a public area. Yard cranes such as RTGC will occupy and block a large section of the access road when they have to travel between stacking yards. As a result, patrol vehicles frequently travel around the yard area to maintain smooth traffic flow.

3.5 Gatehouse

The gatehouse of a container terminal is the first point of physical contact for outbound containers and the last point of physical contact for inbound containers. The efficiency of the gatehouse is of equal importance to that of the quayside and yardside operations. Apart from documentation clearance, usually the gatehouse is also the place to handle issues relating to containers. These include:

- Resolving documentation issues related to containers and tractors and contacting shipping lines, other terminals or other internal departments if necessary;
- Handling dutiable, detention and over-sized containers;
- Collecting charges for chargeable items from drivers;
- Handling of marshalling jobs under gate mode;
- Contacting shipping lines in case of any physical damage or seal-related issues (missing/broken/discrepancy) of the containers;
- Arranging the replacement of damaged empty containers for the drivers;
- Monitoring the waiting time of external tractors;
- Answering enquiries and handling complaints from external parties relating to terminal operation.

The operational flow of external tractors can be described by Figures 3.1 and 3.2

For the terminals in Hong Kong, external tractors will wait at the lay-by area after they complete documentation clearance at the gatehouse. Once the yard operation is ready, the terminal will notify the external tractor driver of the exact location to which the tractor shall go, either though a ticket issued/printed at the lay-by area or by texting the tract driver via SMS. Recently, some terminals like

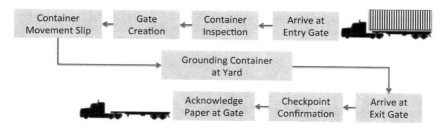

Figure 3.1 Operational flow for collection of import/empty container

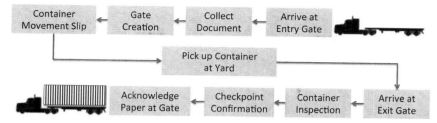

Figure 3.2 Operational flow for delivery of export/empty container

Hong Kong are using mobile apps to inform the tractor drivers of the latest situation, and this has greatly reduced the annoyance of the drivers, as they can keep checking how soon their containers will be handled.[1] Some terminals choose to let the tractors wait at the gatehouse, but this can only be done in those terminals that are not so busy and that have sufficient access road buffers outside the terminals.

When a container arrives at the gatehouse, it is the responsibility of the terminal to inspect the seal and the condition of the container. Similarly, when a container leaves the terminal, it is then the responsibility of the tractor driver to inspect the container. Facilities such as footbridges will be provided at the gatehouse so as to facilitate the inspection of container tops.

3.6 Control tower and planning

The control tower is usually described as the "brain" of a container terminal. It is responsible for the overall control and monitoring of terminal operations. The main functions are categorized under the following sub-systems:

- **Vessel planning** (loading and discharging) – Before the vessel arrives at the terminal, the shipping line will provide the profile and container details of the arriving vessel via electronic data interchange (EDI). The terminal will then start the planning of container discharge and loading work sequence. The sequence is planned with overall consideration of ship stability, port rotation, yard operation efficiency and so forth. Once the planning is completed, the ship planner will go on board to get the approval of the chief officer of the vessel for the overall plan. The work order will then be passed to the control tower via the TOS, and the terminal will start the vessel operations.
- **Yard planning** – The main task of yard planning is to design and plan the yard grounding strategy. Containers from vessel discharge and external tractors are grounded in the stacking yard according to the planned strategy. The strategy must consider the yard utilization and the vessel operation efficiency. Basically, containers with the same or similar attributes are grouped together in the same yard stack. If a container yard is stacked with containers of different attributes, unnecessary container shuffling is required, resulting in low productivity and less cost effectiveness.

- **Berth planning** – Berth planning is responsible for the arrangement of the berthing schedule for all arriving vessels and coordinating with shipping lines on the vessel berthing and departure times. The best berthing arrangement is to strike a balance between the berth utilization rate and the vessel waiting time.
- **Vessel and yard operations control** – The control tower monitors the progress of vessel operation, delivers instructions to frontline operations, coordinates terminal resources deployment and handles unpredictable cases that occur in the terminal. The types of control can be classified into (i) yard operations control and (ii) vessel operations control. For yard operations control, workload distribution among various yard areas is being monitored. In case of heavy yard workload or traffic congestion in a certain yard block, more yard cranes will be deployed to that area, or the workload can be diverted to other blocks. For vessel operations control, the progress of vessel operations will be closely monitored. Operational resources, including quay cranes, yard cranes and tractors, shall be redistributed if there is any deviation from the planned schedule.

3.7 Non-standard containers

Even though the main purpose of using containers is the means of standardizing the transportation, container terminals still have to deal with different kinds of non-standardized operations. Here are some of them:

- **Oversized container** – When there is cargo that exceeds the maximum length and/or width of a container, it will normally be placed on a flat-rack container. This type of container cannot be lifted by the twist-lock mentioned earlier; usually it will be lifted by using wire ropes and slings.
- **Hot box and late come** – All import and export containers are assigned with their respective deadlines for leaving and arriving at the terminal, but there will be a cargo owner and/or shipper who raises a special request for advancing or deferring the deadline. For example, some import containers will be loaded onto external tractors directly so as to reduce time in the entire logistic chain, or some external tractors may defer the gate-in time such that they can go directly to the quayside for loading the export containers. However, this is not a common practice, and only under special circumstances will a container yard allow this to happen.
- **Break-bulk cargo and vehicle** – Occasionally container terminals will also handle break-bulk cargoes, but this is not their preferred business model, as the knowledge and skills are not quite the same. Break-bulk cargo usually requires more space for storage, as it cannot be stacked high, and it may require special (different) types of equipment for handling. For vehicles, the handling is comparatively simple, as they can manoeuvre directly from vessel to landside yard through a gangway ramp. Again, since the vehicles cannot be stacked inside a terminal, they will only be parked temporarily in the yard and will be driven to the depot outside the terminal as soon as possible.

3.8 Safety precautions in container terminals

Safety management in container terminals is a kind of integrated science. Its primary objectives are to (i) advocate a preventive practice to ensure zero accidents and (ii) ensure that loss and injury will be kept minimal in case an accident does happen.

The operations of a container terminal rely substantially on heavy machines that work around the clock. The efficiency of a terminal not only plays a key role in the success of its company but also has a significant impact on the services of the subsequent ports of a vessel and the economy of the city in which the terminal is located. However, regardless of the development of automation, container terminals still require plenty of people in their operation process. That means maintaining a high safety standard is more challenging than thought because of the existence of human factors. The following three aspects are considered the integral parts to terminal safety management:

- **Equipment-based safety** – "Fail-safe design" must be considered during the design and manufacturing stage of the equipment. Preventing accidents is a primary objective even though failure is found in parts of the equipment.
- **Workflow-based safety** – "Risk assessment" shall be carried out when designing not only the tangible elements but also the workflow. This is to ensure that necessary safety measures in all workflows are in place, fully implemented and closely monitored.
- **Behaviour-based safety** – Good working habits and high safety awareness can only be maintained through continuous training and education provided to the personnel.

The three aspects are interrelated in a container terminal's safety management, and a typical container terminal–related accident is always the result of malfunction to any or all aspects mentioned.

In addition, two renowned laws are constantly referenced or cited in terminal safety management, which are:

- **Heinrich's Law** (1931) – In a workplace, for every accident that causes a major injury, there are 29 accidents that cause minor injuries and 300 accidents that cause no injury.
- **Murphy's Law** (Roe, 1952) – anything that can go wrong will go wrong.

The three aspects and the two laws mentioned bring about the following insights:

1. Never neglect the least-frequent accidents.

    People are often prejudiced by the infrequent rate of some accidents and thus believe that things are least likely to happen or even not likely to happen. In fact, this mis-perception could lead to a higher rate of accidents than thought. Cranes in container terminals operate almost on a non-stop basis. For a container terminal with annual throughput of 1 million TEU, the number of lifting actions of all cranes can amount to 300 to 500 times per hour. Although every lift apparently repeats itself in cycles, it is in fact performed in reliance on humans' compliance with a set of workflows and procedures. It is thus this repetitive activity that adds up the small rate of likelihood, and eventually an accident does happen.

2. Fail-safe design must be in place and must not be compromised.

    The more reliance on safety protection provided by the equipment, the less reliance on human decision and judgment. For every post-mortem review of an accident, improvement on equipment safety protection seems to be the most common improvement measure. However, when there is failure in one protective device, some better and more reliable protective devices will be recommended. This is quite an irreversible process. The design of a fail-safe device is to ensure the safety of using the equipment, and this should not be the source of unsafe operation.

3. Workflow-based safety and behaviour-based safety are related to the safety awareness and habits of human beings.

    Both Heinrich's Law and Murphy's Law address the underlying flaw of workflow control and the unsafe behavioural habits of human beings. Human beings are the ultimate goal and reason for having all these safety protections, but they are also the entity responsible for executing these protections. In the end, people's decisions are the foundations for safety to be practiced effectively.

Nevertheless, factors affecting container terminal safety shall not be treated separately or independently, and this is one of the beliefs advocated in this book: that the factors affecting risk management shall be considered holistically.

3.9 Container terminal operations in Hong Kong and China

Logistics is one of the four major industries supporting the economy of Hong Kong, and the intention to develop Hong Kong's logistics industry towards becoming a high-value goods inventory, management and regional distribution center was emphasized in the Chief Executive's Policy Address in 2001. Furthermore, China's National 12th Five-Year Plan, promulgated in March 2011, supports Hong Kong's development into a high-value goods inventory, management and regional distribution center as well as an international maritime center.

Container terminals play a vital role in the logistics value chain. According to the statistics of the World Shipping Council published in 2014, Hong Kong has been among the top three in the 11 years from 2002 to 2012 in terms of annual throughput, and it became world number four in 2013 when Shenzhen surpassed Hong Kong by a slight margin.

The development of the container port industry in China and in Hong Kong has been remarkable in the last two decades. Besides Hong Kong, six other ports in Mainland China are also listed among the top 10 container ports in the world. Referring to Table 1.3, China, as a result, shall be viewed as taking the leading role in the container terminal industry. However, this does not necessarily reflect its capability in risk management.

There have been plenty of major and minor accidents in container terminals throughout the world. Some accidents, which are catastrophic in nature, may cause suspension of business, such as the clashing of quay cranes in Jacksonville, Florida, United States, in September 2008 and the falling of a quay crane in Southampton Docks, U.K., in the same year. The implications of these accidents are multifold. In the short term, they affect revenue owing to the temporary suspension of business. In the long run, such events may lead to an increase in insurance premiums and/or a decrease in company value. Since most investors rely on bank loans for investments in container terminals, a small percentage drop in company value can have a significant impact on shareholders' investment.

Although China is the largest producer of container boxes in the world today, the first shipping container was invented and patented in 1956 by an American named Malcolm McLean (Mayo and Nohria, 2005). Since then, the transportation mode of cargoes, especially for maritime cargoes, has changed drastically. Dedicated container ports, where facilities and equipment are solely designed for container handling, were built starting from 1960s. For Hong Kong, the first container berth has been in operation since 1972. At present, there are altogether 24 dedicated berths for container vessels in Hong Kong. In China, the number of container terminal companies exceeds 300, but the exact number is hard to accurately determine owing to their complicated ownership structures.

Note

1 Hong Kong International Terminals Limited (HIT) worked with three other Kwai-Tsing Terminals and OnePort and launched a mobile app in March 2014. Currently, it consists of the enquiry functions on hot-box estimated delivery time, container details, vessel information, empty collection and return location, inbound tractor appointment and terminal special arrangement, etc.

4 What risks container terminals are facing

4.1 What is risk?

We all face uncertainty in our daily lives. For example, we may not be certain whether we can keep our job tomorrow or whether we can complete any kind of study satisfactorily. Simply speaking, uncertainty is the source of risk. Hubbard (2009) has quoted a short definition of risk from an English dictionary, which is "something bad could happen" (p. 8), and this explains that risk always links to undesirable events that may happen in the future.

Rao and Goldsby (2009) make reference to the works of others in which the "origins of the word 'risk' itself are debated". They quote the suggestions from some researchers that the word "risk" is derived from the Italian word *risicare* (Bernstein, 1996; Khan and Burnes, 2007), which means to dare, while other researchers suggest that the origins of the word "risk" can be traced back to the Arabic word *risq*, which meant "gift from God" (Norrman and Lindroth, 2004).

The notion of risk has never been easy to define for academia. Aven (2012) even uses the term "chaotic" for describing the existing conditions where there exist a vast number of definitions of risk and risk-related concepts (p. 1648). In accounting for the difficulty of coming to a consensus on the notion, Fischhoff and colleagues (1984) in their earlier paper commented that "no definition is advanced as the correct one, because there is no one definition that is suitable for all problems". As a result, the definition of risk, as Fischhoff and colleagues continue, has become "a political choice of the individual resulting from his/her views on the importance of different adverse impacts for a particular situation" (p. 124). In the following paragraphs, a few key definitions advanced or attempted in the literature will be discussed.

March and Shapira (1987) made use of the classical decision theory and defined risk as "variations in the distribution of possible outcomes, their likelihood, and their subjective values" (p. 1404). According to this definition, risk can be viewed as a Cartesian plane with the X-axis being the possible outcomes and the Y-axis being the respective frequency. The "possible outcome" can be viewed as the "consequence" of an event, named "severity" if the outcome is unfavourable. With this concept in mind, any possible outcome can be paired with its corresponding frequency of occurrence. Dividing the frequency by the total number of occurrences can estimate the probability of a particular possible outcome.

Here, the two major elements of risk – **frequency** (or "probability" if divided by the total number of occurrences) and **consequence** (or "severity" if the outcome is negative) – emerge.

Some existing literature relates the term "risk" with uncertainty. One of the examples is a paper written by Al-Bahar and Crandall (1990), who defined risk as the "exposure to the chance of occurrences of events adversely or favourably affecting [project] objectives as a consequence of uncertainty" (p. 534).

In my opinion, risk that may bring positive consequences should be viewed as opportunity, or else the scope of this book will be too broad to come up with a meaningful conclusion. To avoid complication, I adopt the definition of risk that focuses on the **damage that will bring negative consequence to the planned objectives**. This point of view is also advocated by Kaplan and Garrick (1981), who defined risk as uncertainty plus damage. This gives us a clear indication that uncertainty itself does not necessarily lead to risk unless the uncertainty itself will bring detrimental consequences. According to this definition, damage that will certainly happen is not a risk, either, and we shall classify it as an issue rather than a risk.

Wu (2011) provides another expression to the definition of risk that "risks do not exist without a reference to goals, expectations or constraints that are associated with a project". Here, the term "project" is not confined to the traditional definition of project. As we can see today in the business environment, many corporations are trying hard to disintegrate their businesses into various smaller- (but not necessarily small-) scale projects such that these projects will have their own definite goals, expectations and time frame determined by the management. The definition provided by Wu is in fact a much closer and more practical one which can be applied in the real business world.

As per the discussions mentioned, there are different definitions of the term "risk". A more compatible definition will also be adopted for the term "risk" that better covers the problem. Here, the term "risk" is defined as the "potential events that may adversely affect the entity in achieving its objectives". This definition is based on the definition of enterprise risk management (ERM) in the Enterprise Risk Management Framework issued by the Committee of Sponsoring Organizations of the Treadway Commission (COSO) (hereinafter the COSO ERM framework) with slight modifications to suit the SURE model. According to this definition, the risk shall be in the future ("potential") with negative impact ("adversely"), and the consequence shall be with reference to the objectives defined by the entity.

(a) What is operational risk?

Referring to the *Operational Risk Sound Practice Guidance* of the Institute of Operational Risk – "Risk Control Self Assessment" (2010), operational risks are sometimes referred to as "a firm's intrinsic or inherent potential exposure and in addition to the internal environment, . . . should consider factors arising from the external environment including industry trends as well as taking into account any 'upstream' or newly emerging risks" (p. 6). The term "inherent" can be further explained by the COSO ERM framework such that "inherent risk is the risk to an entity in the absence of any actions management might take to alter either the risk's likelihood or impact" (p. 47).

Apart from this definition, the Basel Committee defines operational risk as "the risk of loss resulting from inadequate or failed internal processes, people and systems or from external events". This definition includes legal risk but excludes strategic and reputational risk. According to the Guidelines on Operational Risk Management (National Bank and Finanzmarkt, 2006) issued by Oesterreichische National Bank of Austria, operational risk is defined as "the risk of loss resulting from inadequate or failed internal processes, people and systems or from external events, and includes legal risk" (p. 9). These two definitions are mainly formulated for regulating financial institutions. They give the reader general understanding of operational risk, but their application in the container terminal business may not be entirely appropriate.

Davies and colleagues (2006), on the other hand, suggest that operational risk "can be defined as the risk of loss resulting from inadequate or failed processes, systems, human performance or external events" (p. 2). This definition is comparatively generic in nature and is relatively more applicable to the description of risk management practices in the container terminal business. Nevertheless, referring to the introductory page of *Operational Risk Governance* issued by the Institute of Operational Risk – "Operational Risk Sound Practice Guidance, September 2010", "there is no one-size-fits-all approach to the management of operational risk. However by drawing on the experience of practicing risk professionals it is possible to identify examples of good practice . . ." That is to say, effectively, the definition of operational risk may best be defined by the organization itself, as it is the one that understands its situations the most.

Operational risks as applied here mainly focus on those relating to the container terminal industry. Unfortunately, other than a handful of literature that discusses the operational flow of the container terminal industry, there is virtually no literature which appropriately explains what major operational risks the terminals are facing and how they respond to those risks. Therefore, our own findings are required in developing the analysis framework.

(b) Two major elements of risk

Referring to the discussion of March and Shapira's definition of risk, there are two major elements in any risk item – **frequency** (or "probability" if divided by the total number of occurrence) and **consequence** (or "severity" if the outcome is negative). In this section, we are going to review these two elements in detail.

Kaplan and Garrick refer to frequency as the outcome of an experiment of some kind involving repeated trials, and therefore it is a hard, measurable number. The experiment here, as Kaplan and Garrick explained, can be a thought experiment or an experiment to be done in the future.

Kaplan and Garrick define probability as a "number used to communicate a state of mind. It is subjective and not measurable, at least not in the usual way".

The main concept here is that for probability, we can compare that one event is more likely than the other, but we may not necessary get an **objective** measurement of the actual occurrences. However, we have to be careful about the differences between frequency and probability, although they are sometimes used interchangeably in risk analysis.

In practical application, frequency and probability do co-exist in risk management. When there are sufficient historical data concerning the occurrence of a particular risk item, then the frequency of this occurrence will normally be used in the risk analysis. Otherwise, the chance of occurrence will have to be based on some theoretical calculations, that is, probability. However, because of limited resources in the business world, historical data may only exist in part of the problem, and therefore a combination of frequency and probability may be required in real-life application.

The term "consequence" adopted in this book refers to the negative consequence of an outcome. For negative consequences, Li and Cullinane (2003) define severity as the "outcome of a materialized hazard and is quantifiable in the sense that it can be expressed in monetary terms" (p. 269). For a container port, a high-severity risk item can be considered a big incident such as suspension of business or fatal accidents that cause substantial loss of revenue and shareholders' value. Lewis (2003) further explains that the negative consequences are "determined by some function of internal (operational) and external (customer) losses", and the risk-analysis process shall "consider different layers of loss: operational; customer; direct stakeholder; and, generic stakeholder" (p. 219). This means that the analysis of risk and its consequences should take all stakeholders into consideration so as to provide a full picture. Superficial analysis with only a single layer of loss may render the result useless in some cases.

The term "**stakeholder**", mentioned earlier, is important because the same risk may result in significantly different consequences for different stakeholders. Kaplan and Garrick discussed the relativity of risk such that the risk itself is relative to the observer, and therefore it is subjective. That is to say, for the same risk, different people (or entities) will assess it differently, and therefore they may have different acceptance levels and mitigation measures towards the same risk item. This concept is important in real-life applications. In carrying out risk assessment, different people (or entities) may come up with different decisions, and this is considered normal based on this concept.

Relativity plays an important role in this book, as one of the objectives is to analyse demographically how different container terminals consider and respond to similar risk items. Through this analysis, the differences in risk considerations are revealed, and the respective risk responses can be useful for investors, in particular the shareholders aboard, to understand the risk-management culture and to formulate the best strategy.

In most of the literature, risk is defined as "probability times consequence" or "probability times severity" (Li and Cullinane, 2003). However, Kaplan and Garrick raised the argument that risk is probability and consequence but not the probability times consequence that most people get used to. The main reason for establishing this argument is that in the case of a single scenario, the "times" may mislead the readers to equate a low-probability, high-damage scenario with a high-probability, low-damage scenario. The argument made by Kaplan is not wrong, but it is difficult to apply in risk analysis, and therefore it is seldom used in real-life situations.

4.2 Risk in container terminals

From an academic point of view, much of the literature concerning the container terminal industry tends to be associated with the operating systems so as to improve the efficiency of a container terminal (Cullinane et al., 2006) and use of latest technology and equipment (Steenken and Stahlbock, 2004; Vis and De Koster, 2003). One area that has received little attention and yet is an important one in the management of container terminals is how to manage risk. There is virtually no research in relation to risk management of container terminals. Though container terminals spend tens of millions of dollars each year in risk management in order to minimize their risk exposure, there is no scientific evidence demonstrating whether these resources are spent adequately or appropriately.

In order to satisfy statutory requirements, most container terminals in Mainland China have their own safety departments, with the main focus on arranging safety training, administering safety protection equipment and tools, performing safety inspections and handling "postmortems" of accidents. There is actually little specific research that focuses on the operational risk of terminal operations, and thus no structured risk-management strategies, systems and tools have been developed. The literatures reviewed can only give a direction on how to carry out risk evaluation from the general perspectives. With the increasing importance of container terminals in the Asia-Pacific region, it is not reasonable to ignore the impact of the highly disruptive events that might occur throughout the operations.

A study in relation to risk and safety management of container terminals has been carried out previously in Taiwan (Shang and Tseng, 2010), but there have been virtually no similar studies carried out in the mainland or in Hong Kong. As mentioned earlier, this is not in line with Hong Kong and China's leading positions in the container terminal industry in terms of annual container throughput. This research, as a result, could be a starting point for the long-term systematic analysis of risk management for container terminals not only in Hong Kong and China but also in Asia and all over the world.

According to a survey carried out in the United States in 1982 concerning the industry-wide cost of risk as a percentage of revenue (Boodman, 1987), the figure for the transportation industry was the highest among 34 industries surveyed; its cost at 2.37% was about five times the average value of 0.48% and was about twice as much as the second-highest industry (health care, 1.29%). The cost of business risk here included administrative costs, insurance premiums and unreimbursed losses. The captioned survey was carried out more than 30 years ago, but without any major breakthrough in the transportation mode (such as manless driving) during the last few decades, the author believes transportation is still the most risky industry in terms of the cost of risk against its revenue.

The risks related to the container terminal industry can be disastrous and catastrophic. In 2003, Busan port of South Korea was badly damaged by a typhoon. Eleven quayside gigantic cranes collapsed and could not be repaired. This disaster not only caused material loss in terms of damaged equipment and quay structure but also the loss of business to competitors. According to the author's estimate, the loss caused by this incident could be as high as HKD 1 billion.

With the unlimited number of risks the container terminals are facing, the author, based on his 20+ years of experience with the industry and the comments from various senior managers of container terminal companies, has summarized these risks into six major categories for this study. They are as follows.

(a) Natural disaster

Natural disaster includes the risk associated with acts of God, such as typhoon, earthquake, tsunami, flood and so forth. This kind of risk is not initiated by human beings, and usually it is not predictable. As the consequences can sometimes be devastating, some of these risks are considered "force majeure" and are excluded from many insurance policies. As a result, the insured may have to bear the risk and its consequences themselves.

(b) Accident caused by external event

"External event" refers to the incidents **unintentionally** caused by a person or a party other than the container terminal company itself and its contractors. For example, a vessel collides with the quay structure or a car crashes into the terminal gatehouse. This kind of risk is caused by human beings, and prior planning for such accidents is not possible; the people involved have no employment relationship with the company concerned. Incidents caused by customers such as shipping companies shall also be classified in this category.

(c) Accident caused by staff

This kind of risk is caused by the staff directly or indirectly employed by the container terminal company concerned—for example, the falling of stacked containers caused by mis-operation by an equipment operator, regardless of whether the operator is employed by the company or by its contractor. The consequence of this kind of risk is more imminent in nature. When a staff member has induced this kind of risk, the company, other than bearing the financial consequences of the risk, might be subject to legal liabilities as well.

(d) Breakdown/failure of equipment

The operation of a container terminal involves plenty of equipment such as ship-to-shore cranes, gantry cranes, forklifts and the like. The breakdown of equipment is unavoidable even when there are good preventive maintenance systems in place. Once a piece of equipment breaks down, it is not easy to find a replacement immediately, especially for the ship-to-shore crane. The consequence of this kind of risk is the high repair and maintenance cost and the frequent complaints from customers, which may eventually cause loss of business.

(e) Breakdown/failure of information technology (IT) system

The operation of modernized container terminals relies heavily on the IT system to improve efficiency, reduce manpower and communicate with other parties, such as customers and Customs. With the vast volume of containers to be handled per day, the breakdown of the IT system in a modernized container terminal can be disastrous. IT system reliability and security, as a result, is one of the major areas for risk management in container terminals.

(f) Social and human issues

Apart from accidents induced by staff as mentioned in point (c), people working in a container terminal can cause another type of risk which is not directly related to the daily operation of the workers, but the remuneration and working conditions of the workers and the threat itself are planned actions instead of unintentional accidents. Referring to Point (e), even with a sophisticated IT system in place, a container terminal still requires hundreds, if not thousands, of workers such as stevedores, checkers, crane operators, tractor drivers and more to support the operations. Labour unions, as a result, are not uncommon in sizeable container terminals, nor are strikes. The existence of labour unions therefore poses a significant threat to operations, and their acts are separated from unintentional accidents as defined in Point (c).

Because of lack of proper understanding and review of individual risk items, a company sometimes may mismanage risks by committing three different kinds of errors, explained in the following paragraphs.

One kind of mismanagement is the absence of any strategy to deal with risk items whose potential for occurrence is high. For example, there are pretty high chances of super-typhoons a few times in a decade at the location of the terminal, but the design of the crane and its supporting structure have not taken this into account.

The second kind of mismanagement relates to spending of resources on incidents that stand a very low chance of occurrence. For instance, a container terminal has spent a substantial amount of resources on reducing the damages caused by a tsunami, but the location of the terminal is not close to an earthquake-prone area or the open sea, and there is no precedent or likelihood of occurrence in the past (for example, a river terminal).

The third type has to do with arriving at a correct response to a risk but following some faulty assumptions. This situation is similar to the Type III error described by Mosteller (1948) that it "correctly rejects the null hypothesis for the wrong reason". Transforming this concept into operational risk management of a container terminal, this Type III error can be assumed as adopting an appropriate response to a particular risk item, but the reasons to arrive at this response is not correct or appropriate, or at least it is not based on the same considerations as most of the terminal operators. For example, a container terminal may spend millions of dollars on installing a lightning-protection system for the sake of ensuring reliability, but in fact the fundamental issue for providing this protection shall be the protection of the people inside or in the vicinity of the cranes.

In view of the amount of resources involved, it may not be easy for a container terminal company to consolidate the historical data for each of the risk items. For some particular risk items in container terminal operational risk management, data collection can be impractical. For example, the frequency of a catastrophic crane accident cannot be determined if there has been no such accident before, but the probability of having such an accident is hardly believed to be absolute zero.

Type III error for operational risk management has no substantial detrimental or imminent effects on an organization. However, management frequently committing Type III error may have a wrong perception of competency in formulating risk-management strategy. And when the situation changes, they may easily commit other types of errors in the future.

5 Risk management concept and theory

5.1 Risk management

Risk management has been a hot topic in academic fields in the last few decades, especially after the occurrence of catastrophic accidents and major financial crises, such as the Chernobyl nuclear power plant disaster in 1986 and the dot-com bubble in 1997 to 2000. In reality, similar risks have repeatedly occurred even though the causes and the extent of damage may not be exactly the same. During the last 5 years, we have encountered the financial tsunami in 2008 and the accident in Fukushima I Nuclear Power Plant in 2011. Risk management, as a result, is one of the key issues that most entities today are dealing with in their daily operations.

(a) Why risk management?

Risk management, as can be interpreted from the words directly, is the way of handling uncertainties that may lead to detrimental consequences. Interestingly, Hubbard (2009) uses a simple phrase to describe the purpose of risk management, which is "being smart about taking chances" (p. 10). On the other hand, Paté-Cornell (2012) has defined risk management as "involves by definition decisions under uncertainty that can be addressed by decision analysis" (p. 1828).

Sung (2005) defines risk management as an integration of limited resources to lower deleterious effects. Here, the resource factor is taken into consideration in risk management. This is the result of the fact that we will not have an infinite amount of resources in terms of people, money, time and the like, and, sensibly, we will not reduce the risk to our acceptance level **at any cost**. To strike a balance is the most important element, and also the art, in risk management.

Haimes and colleagues (2002) define risk management as part of the eight-phase methodology for managing risk that involves "identification of management options for dealing with the filtered scenarios, and estimating the cost, performance benefits, and risk reduction of each" (p. 383). The definition provided by Haimes and colleagues suits their developed eight-phase methodology, but in general this may confuse the readers who believe that risk management represents the whole management process rather than one step/phase of it.

Nevertheless, the risk management definitions advocated by Sung and Haimes and colleagues address both the cost and resource factors. From a management point of view, risk management means to reduce and contain the risk to an acceptable level by using a reasonable amount of resources in terms of people, money, time and so forth such that it does not substantially reduce the chance of achieving the pre-determined goals and objectives. This definition for risk management is adopted.

Shang and Tseng (2010) consider that the main purpose of risk management is to develop systems for controlling risk. They advise that businesses measure the likely damage frequency and severity, take advance preventive measures and emphasize the risk in financial management.

Ward (2003) states that the purpose of risk management is "to improve organizational performance via systematic identification, appraisal and management of risks to that performance" (p. 16). Note that the definition here emphasizes improvement, meaning that risk management itself should be able to provide some enhancement to the organization in terms of its performance, and this is considered among the "theoretical benefits" of risk management. However, according to March and Shapira (1987), managers are "quite insensitive to estimates of the probabilities of possible outcomes; their decisions are particularly affected by the way their attention is focused on critical performance targets" (p. 1404). According to my personal observations in the container terminal industry, these decisions do not necessarily factor in risk management properly. This results in a performance gap in risk management, and thus it is one of the main purposes of developing a proper risk-management strategy.

As discussed, no entity is able to provide an unlimited supply of resources, and therefore the purpose of risk management, as the author has experienced when working with container terminals, is effectively an art of balancing the risk acceptance level and the amount of resources that can be utilized.

(b) Risk management process

There is plenty of literature which describes the process of risk management, and the descriptions are very similar in nature. For example, Eloff and colleagues (1993) describe risk management as a continuous cycle comprising five major components, including risk identification, risk analysis, risk assessment, risk resolution and risk monitoring. This model is relatively simple and generic enough for paving the path of the model. However, two components – risk analysis and risk assessment – are sometimes combined into one by other researchers such as Leung and colleagues (2003).

Another risk-management model developed by Tummala and Mak (2001) consists of five core elements, including risk identification, risk measurement, risk assessment, risk evaluation and risk monitoring. This model is very similar to the five-component risk-management process of Eloff and colleagues, while some other literature may combine risk measurement and risk assessment into risk analysis. Likewise, Al-Bahar and Crandall (1990) proposed a new model named the construction risk management system, which consists of four processes, including risk identification, risk analysis and evaluation, response management and system administration. Both models are effectively derived from the same process flow, and the major difference between these models is how different processes are demarcated.

Based on the various models discussed, it is concluded that a crucial part of risk management is risk analysis, even though this may be called by various names. Without a proper understanding of the nature of risk, the management may not be able to deal with the risk adequately.

It is more appropriate to start with the model that can be found in the COSO ERM Framework. According to this framework, ERM is

> a process, effected by an entity's board of directors, management and other personnel, applied in strategy setting and across the enterprise, designed to identify potential events that may affect the entity, and manage risk to be within the entity's risk appetite, to provide reasonable assurance regarding the achievement of entity objectives. (COSO, 2004, p. 6)

Since this study is to be carried out in a business environment, the ERM framework is a suitable model for further elaboration.

The ERM proposed under this framework consists of eight interrelated components, which are internal environment, objective setting, event identification, risk assessment, risk response, control activities, information and communication and monitoring. In the COSO ERM Framework, there are already ample definitions for each of the eight components, and therefore these are not repeated.

The study of all eight components under the COSO ERM Framework could be too broad and complicated for this book and may require a tremendous amount of resources for understanding the internal process (internal environment) and the core values (objective setting) of an entity. To cope with this, this book will only focus on event identification, risk assessment and risk response.

The components described refer to the risk-management process, but the risk-management process may be of minimal use if it does not meet the objectives of the entity. As such, the COSO ERM Framework creates another dimension in the model so as to ensure the objectives are clearly identified well before the execution of the process and are consistent with the entity's risk appetite. These objectives can be classified into four main categories: strategic, operations, reporting and compliance. Operational risk is the main area of study, and therefore we will focus mainly on the operations category under this model.

A third dimension depicted in the COSO ERM Framework is the relationship between the target entity and its organization as a whole. Depending on what organizational unit the target entity belongs to, there are four major categories in this dimension: subsidiary, business unit, division and entity level. The introduction of this dimension is to allow the target entity to be applicable in various levels of an organization, and this is particularly useful for large business conglomerates,

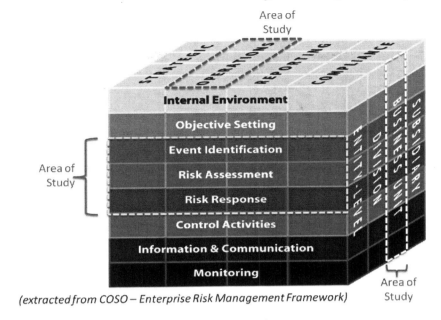

(extracted from COSO – Enterprise Risk Management Framework)

Figure 5.1 Components in COSO ERM framework

as the risk management objectives and risk appetites may not be the same at different levels of an organization. The business unit category would be the main focus, as most of the container terminals operating in Hong Kong and in the mainland are effectively independent business units, even though there may be similarities in shareholding structures. Figure 5.1 highlights the components of the COSO ERM Framework that the book targets.

As per the discussions on various risk-management processes mentioned earlier, risk analysis has been used as one of the components in the process, while some other streams of literature use the term "risk analysis" at the same (or even higher) status as "risk management". A good example is the definition by the Society of Risk Analysis that

> Risk analysis is broadly defined to include risk assessment, risk characterization, risk communication, risk management, and policy relating to risk, in the context of risks of concern to individuals, public- and private-sector organizations, and to society at a local, regional, national, or global level. (Society of Risk Analysis, www.sra.org/about-society-risk-analysis)

According to this definition, risk analysis covers almost the whole process, and risk management becomes only an element in the risk analysis. To avoid confusion, we try not to adopt this term "risk analysis" even though we sometimes may have to use it when quoting other researchers.

(c) Event identification

Referring to the COSO ERM Framework, an event is defined as "an incident or occurrence emanating from internal or external sources that may affect implementation of strategy or achievement of objectives" (COSO, 2004, p. 38). However, the "time" factor is not well addressed in this definition, as we usually refer to an "event" (also in the Oxford Dictionary) as something that is happening or will most probably happen. An incident that will never happen, as in the case of some potential risks with low probability, will be difficult for general people to accept as an "event". Again referring to the COSO ERM Framework, "events with a potentially negative impact represent risks, which require management's assessment and response" (COSO, 2004, p. 38). The definition here echoes the discussions in Chapter 4, Section 4.01, about the difference between an issue and a risk. The words "event" and "issue", as described in this book, are essentially neutral (as they can be both good and bad) in terms of the consequences they are to bring. Although the COSO ERM Framework has used the term "event", for clarity, we will use another term, "risk item", to represent the incident that may result in detrimental consequences for the entity.

Management has to deal with thousands of risk items which cannot be ascertained in terms of chances of occurrence and level of consequences. As suggested by Morgan and colleagues (2000), with thousands of specific hazards (risk items) faced by the management, grouping risks into a manageable number of categories is unavoidable (p. 49). Furthermore, the COSO ERM Framework has illustrated one of the approaches in categorizing the risk items (events) based on internal and external factors (COSO, 2004, p. 44).

Techniques which are commonly used for risk item (event) identification have been described in the COSO ERM Framework (COSO, 2004, p. 41), including event inventories, internal analysis, escalation or threshold triggers, facilitated workshop and interviews, leading event indicators, loss event data methodologies and process flow analysis. Details of each technique are not discussed in this literature review, as they can be found directly in the COSO ERM Framework.

(d) Risk assessment

Once the risk item is identified, the next step according to the COSO Framework is to assess the risk item itself. Al-Bahar and Crandall advocate a seven-component model for risk analysis (assessment) which starts with "data collection", and is then separated into two parallel paths including "objective statistical data" and "subjective judgmental data". When these two processes are completed, the next component is "modelling uncertainty". Thereafter, the process is again divided into two independent processes, which are "assessment of potential consequences" and "assessment of probability distribution". When these two assessments are done, the last component is "evaluation of potential impact of risk". Apart from simply assessing the probability and severity of a risk item, this model emphasizes the data-collection stage of the assessment, including both objective and subjective data, and this also echoes the previous discussion regarding the relativity of the risk item.

It has been common knowledge that likelihood and impact are the two main perspectives to be investigated in risk assessment. This is also reinforced in the COSO ERM Framework (COSO, 2004, p. 47). When analysis takes place, the term "likelihood" is often replaced by the term "frequency" or "probability", while "severity" and "consequence" are often used instead of "impact". These two perspectives have been discussed in the preceding section. However, to simplify the discussion, we use "probability" and "severity" as the two main perspectives in risk assessment, even though they also carry the intrinsic meanings of frequency and consequence.

The most common risk-assessment tool used by managements is the risk matrix. A risk matrix is a two-dimensional representation of risk elements, with one axis being the severity and the other axis being the probability. It is also called a "bi-criteria assessment" according to Haimes and colleagues (2002). According to the relative severity and probability, the area under the graph can be sub-divided into several regions, say from very high risk to very low. For example, the region having risk items with very high severity and very high probability are classified as "high-risk region". Based on the severity and the probability of a particular risk item, it can be marked as a single point on the graph. If this single point is located within the high-risk region, the respective risk item is paid high attention. A graphical representation of a typical risk matrix is shown in Figure 5.2. Any particular risk item can be represented by a node with coordinate (S_i, P_i) in the risk matrix, simply referred to as the risk coordinate.

Generic Risk Matrix

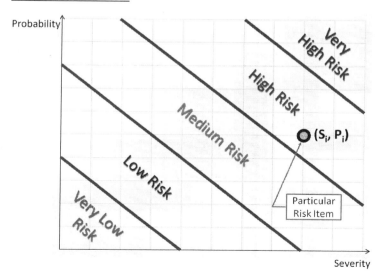

Figure 5.2 A typical risk matrix

The risk matrix is not the only technique used in risk assessment. For example, Hubbard (2009) has described in his book *The Failure of Risk Management: Why It's Broken and How to Fix It* how the Monte Carlo model can be applied in risk assessment. This Monte Carlo model, together with other similar models, is based on calibrated probabilities to express the uncertainties of a particular risk item. However, these kind of models are too complicated, as they involve tremendous amounts of data collection, assumptions and numerical calculations for one particular risk item, and therefore they are not adopted.

In this study, the concept of the risk matrix with incorporation of the risk coordinate is used as the tool for communicating risk levels with the respondents (participants), as it is widely accepted and is being used by most of the risk-management stakeholders. To facilitate our analysis, the risk matrix to be used is systematically divided into fixed intervals so as to assist the respondents in answering our interview questions.

(e) Risk response

Referring to Figure 5.1, risk response is the last component in the risk-management process studied in the model. Simply speaking, risk response is how an entity acts towards an identified risk item. According to the COSO ERM Framework, "effective ERM requires that management select a response that is expected to bring risk likelihood and impact within the entity's risk tolerance" (COSO, 2004, p. 11). There are four kinds of responses as described by COSO, which are avoidance, reduction, sharing and acceptance.

Avoidance is taking any action to prevent the entity from having the risk item occur. Reduction is lowering the likelihood (probability) and/or the negative consequence (severity) of a risk item. Sharing is reducing the risk by transferring a portion of the risk to a third party such as an insurance company, and both the likelihood (probability) and/or the negative consequence (severity) could be transferred as well. The main difference between reduction and sharing is that sharing does not affect (or diminish) the nature of the risk itself but constitutes just a transfer of part or all of the risk to others. Acceptance means taking no action at all and absorbing the risk internally.

Similar classifications exist in other literature as well. Tummala and Mak (2001) proposed five categories in their risk-control (response) approach, namely, avoid, reduce, accept, spread and transfer. Here, the fourth approach, "spread", according to Tummala and Mak (2001, p 127), is to "modify the situation or take remedial actions to lower the risk severity and/or risk probability level, and to accept the associated risk". Referring to the definition from the COSO ERM Framework, this "spread" approach is effectively similar to "reduce", and therefore it may confuse users if both "reduce" and "spread" share similar meaning.

Al-Bahar and Crandall's (1990) five strategies in the risk-management framework are slightly different from those mentioned and include risk avoidance, loss reduction and risk prevention, risk retention, risk transfer (non-insurance) and

Risk Response in Graphical Representation

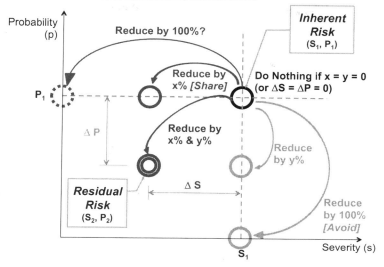

Figure 5.3 Graphical representation of different risk responses

insurance. However, the demarcation lines between these strategies are not clearly and precisely defined. For example, it may be hard to differentiate between loss reduction and risk transfer. As a result, it is better to follow the classification as proposed in the COSO ERM Framework, with slight modifications.

Based on these discussions and making use of a generic risk matrix, a graphical representation of different risk responses has been developed (Figure 5.3). This figure introduces two new terms, inherent risk and residual risk. According to the COSO ERM Framework, inherent risk is "the risk to an entity in the absence of any actions management might take to alter either the risk's likelihood or impact", while residual risk is "the risk that remains after management responds to the risk" (COSO, 2004, p. 47).

Referring to Figure 5.3, inherent risk and residual risk can be represented by two nodes on the graph with coordinates (S_1, P_1) and (S_2, P_2), respectively. The differences between the two coordinates, represented by ΔS and ΔP, correlate to the risk response of the management. The two percentages, x% and y%, represent the change in risk status of the inherent risk and can further be represented numerically by:

$$x\% = \Delta S \ / \ S_1 \text{ and } y\% = \Delta P \ / \ P_1$$

This concept be named the **"Risk Node Coordinate"** concept.

By making use of the COSO ERM Framework with slight modification, five instead of four risk responses can be illustrated by ΔS and ΔP under the graph.

For the **"accept"** or "do nothing" risk response strategy, (S_2, P_2) will be equal to (S_1, P_1). That is, ΔS and ΔP are both 0.

If the probability of the particular risk item is reduced from P_1 to 0 ($\Delta P = P_1$, or y = 100), that means the particular risk will never happen after the risk response is applied. Practically, this is equivalent to the **"avoid"** response.

By imposing safeguard measures such as insurance, the severity of a particular risk item is reduced by x%, and ΔS is not equal to 0. This response can be classified as **"share"**.

If probability of a particular risk item is reduced by y% and thus ΔP is not 0, it means some measures have been applied such that the probability of the inherent risk is diminished, and this is in fact the **"reduce"** response.

Reduction of severity and reduction of probability are not mutually exclusive, since ΔS and ΔP can both be greater than 0 simultaneously. For example, for ship impact risk, we may reduce the severity by having insurance coverage, while at the same time, we can reduce the probability of occurrence by enforcing more stringent policies for vessel berthing (such as deploying additional tugboats). When this situation exists, both the probability and the severity of the inherent risk are reduced. There is no particular term to address this risk response in the COSO ERM Framework. For simplicity, this dual-action response is treated as **"reduce both"**.

Theoretically, severity is never eliminated (i.e., reduced by 100%) as long as the risk does happen. This can be explained by the formula "Risk = Hazard / Safeguards" derived by Kaplan and Garrick (1981). Here, "safeguards" are defined as the "means or device to reduce the risk" (p. 12). The implication of this formula is that since "safeguard" cannot be infinite, the risk therefore can never be reduced to 0, and thus, theoretically, we are not able to eliminate a risk by simply imposing safeguard measures. By the same token, the node that shows 100% reduction in severity is marked with dotted line to distinguish the possibility of non-existence.

The graphical representation of risk response in Figure 5.3 forms the basic idea for risk-response classification. With this graph in place, participants in the interviews (in this study, management of container terminals) found it easier to quantify their inherent and residual risks from a particular risk item. Through the discussion, we have defined five response strategies with respect to the COSO ERM Framework, namely, accept, avoid, share, reduce and reduce both. These five risk-response strategies are adopted in the current study.

5.2 Risk evaluation and derivation of SURE model

In the previous section, the discussion was mainly based on the COSO ERM Framework, which primarily focuses on how risks should be managed and how they should be assessed. There is a lot of literature and numerous theories that can be utilized to explain how people make decisions on event identification, risk assessment and risk response (collectively referred to henceforth as risk evaluation) as part of the risk-management process, which is situated in a complex business environment that includes the need to represent the interests of stakeholders.

The Theory of Planned Behaviour and the Protective Action Decision Model are used to develop a new model used to analyse risk evaluation by managers of container terminals. Further description of these models is provided in the subsequent sections.

(a) Theory of Planned Behaviour (TPB)

The Theory of Planned Behaviour (TPB) originates from the Theory of Reasoned Action (TRA), which was first introduced by Ajzen and Fishbein in 1975 (cited in Madden et al., 1992). TRA is a model posited to explain (or predict) a specific form of behaviour. According to Madden and colleagues, "behavioural intentions, which are the immediate antecedents of behaviour, are a function of salient information or beliefs about the likelihood that performing a particular behaviour will lead to a specific outcome" (1992, p. 3).

According to the theorists, many different types of behaviours are planned behaviours, caused by a particular attention (behavioural intention). A behavioural intention is shaped by three antecedents, namely, attitude, subjective norm and behavioural control.

Attitude is the sum of beliefs about a particular behaviour weighted by evaluations of these beliefs. Eagly and Chaiken (1993) published the book *The Psychology of Attitudes* and defined attitude as "a psychological tendency that is expressed by evaluating a particular entity with some degree of favor or disfavor" (p. 1). Loyalty, honesty and patriotism are examples of attitude.

The subjective norm comes from the influence of the people in one's social environment and in particular their beliefs and opinions, each weighted with a specific degree of importance. That influence affects an individual in making decisions or having a certain kind of behaviour. For example, the Chinese tend to save more money than do Americans, and this could be the result of many other Chinese saving substantial amounts as well. This TRA model can be presented by a path model diagram (Figure 5.4).

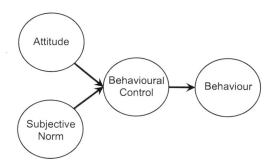

Figure 5.4 Path model for Theory of Reasoned Action (TRA)
(Source: Madden et al., 1992)

To further explain this theory, Hale and colleagues (2003, p. 260) simplified the model with a formula:

$$BI = (AB)W_1 + (SN)W_2$$

where
BI = behavioural intention
AB = one's attitude toward performing the behaviour
W = empirically derived weights
SN = one's subjective norm related to performing the behaviour

This formula is a supplement to the graphical representation of the theory. In reality, the factors (W_1) are unique in every situation, and therefore it is difficult to generalize this formula for a wider range of applications.

According to Hale and colleagues (2003, p. 260), a subjective norm is "a person's belief about whether significant others feel that he or she should perform the target behaviour". Here, the two definitions of subjective norm mainly focus on the **subjective views** of others, and these subjective views are difficult to identify and/or measure, since there can be vastly different opinions from different people even for a particular risk item in any business unit. The new model advances this concept by **using the industry norm in place of the subjective norm**.

Ajzen (1991) extended the boundary condition of pure volitional control specified in the TRA and developed TPB. Apart from the two elements – attitude and subjective norm – in TRA, a new element named perceived behavioural control is introduced in TPB. This is based on the assumption that perceived behavioural control, which can be explained as how the decision makers see the effectiveness of their decisions, affects behavioural intention, thus affecting the behaviour.

Madden and colleagues (1992, p. 4) further explained the perceived behavioural control with the observation that "the more resources and opportunities individuals think they possess, the greater should be their perceived behavioural control over the behaviour". Referring to Madden and colleagues, this TPB model is schematically represented in the diagram shown in Figure 5.5.

Since the development of TPB, many other research works and models have used TPB as the foundation, such as the "Risk Information Seeking and Processing Model" developed by Griffin and colleagues (1999), "Predicting User Intentions: Comparing the Technology Acceptance Model with the Theory of Planned Behaviour" by Mathieson (1991) and "Gender and Age Differences in Employee Decisions about New Technology: An Extension to the Theory of Planned Behaviour" by Morris and colleagues (2005). However, it is not the intention of this book to review all models and developments in relation to TPB. On the other hand, the three elements in TPB are important in developing the new model, although the nomenclature may be different and the elements may be further divided into sub-elements for analysis. As will be discussed later, part of the TPB developed by Ajzen is incorporated in the model.

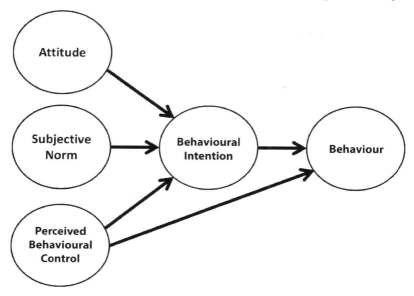

Figure 5.5 Path model for the Theory of Planned Behaviour (TPB)
(Source: Madden et al., 1992)

(b) Protection Action Decision Model (PADM)

TPB focuses mainly on the actions to be taken by individuals. If the actions to be taken affect more than just the individuals who make the decisions, TPB becomes inadequate, especially when there are other factors to be considered when making a decision, such as the resources available in the group. Furthermore, the subjective norm in TPB mainly concerns how the other parties act (the action), but that does not take into account how a third party thinks (the perception). Here we need another model to supplement the deficiency of TPB when dealing with the risk-response decision in this study.

The Protection Action Decision Model (PADM) was recently developed by Lindell and Perry (2012) and is a multi-stage model that "identifies three core perceptions – threat perception, protective action perception, and stakeholder perception – that form the basis for decisions about how to respond to an imminent or long-term threat" (p. 616).

As explained by Lindell and Perry, the two main attributes of threat perception are probability and consequence ("severity"). These two attributes have been discussed in detail in previous sections. According to Bubeck and colleagues (2012), high threat perception does not necessarily lead to mitigation measures (p. 1493). That is to say, the risk-response consideration is not limited to probability and severity of the risk itself.

Protective action perception refers to the anticipated result of the risk-response measures. Lindell and Perry summarized their earlier findings, which can be further divided into hazard-related attributes and resource-related attributes. Hazard-related attributes consider the efficacy and usefulness of the measures, as well as their subsequent implications. For example, to prevent a vessel colliding with a terminal, some ports impose regulations that the vessels shall be escorted by tugboat when close to the port area. However, these measures do not totally eliminate the chance of a similar accident, as the vessel may lose control or the mooring rope may break.

Resource-related attributes mainly concern cost, skill and time requirements of the measures to be implemented. The insurance premium is certainly a kind of resource-related attribute, but there are other related costs such as administration costs for handling insurance contracts and claims. The talent and experience of the staff (say, in handling insurance contracts and claims) are also resource-related attributes. If the company does not possess the necessary talents, it could be worse off when it has insurance in place (for example, double insurance).

For stakeholder perception, Lindell and Perry emphasize the interrelationships among stakeholders, determined by their power over each other's decisions to adopt risk-response measures. The stakeholders here refer to the entities that must be taken into account when choosing the risk response, and this may include authorities, customers, shareholders, management, employees and so forth.

(c) Stakeholder Uniplanar Risk Evaluation (SURE) model

With reference to the foregoing discussion, there are three elements in TPB, namely, attitude, subjective norm and perceived behavioural control, and another three perceptions of PADM, namely, threat perception, protective action perception and stakeholder perception. These six constructs are not mutually exclusive, and some of them overlap with each other in terms of their meanings. For example, perceived behavioural control may include the protective action perception. A simple combination of the two may not lead to an effective model that can allow users to understand the entire situation.

By drawing on TPB and PADM, I have developed a new model which can be used to explain the risk-evaluation (RE) behaviour of container terminal managers, summarized in the schematic representation in Figure 5.6. In this tree diagram, the attributes of the risk-evaluation process are first divided into two main streams, risk specific and stakeholder specific. The risk specific stream is further divided into risk perception and protective action perception sub-streams. In risk perception, the two attributes are probability and severity, originating from the PADM. Similarly for the protective action perception sub-stream, the two major attributes from the PADM are perceived cost (resource related) and perceived efficacy (hazard related).

[Note: There have been some debates on the use of the word "attribute" when the SURE model was being developed. To avoid confusion, here we assume the term "attribute" has the same meaning as the "shaper", which can be described as the factors that affect the decision to be made. Further evaluation of this term is recommended in future studies.]

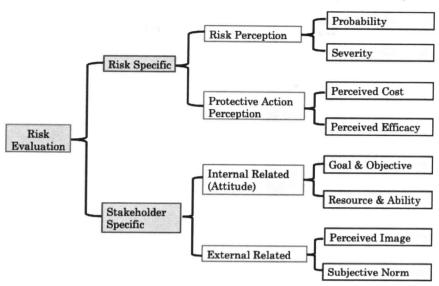

Figure 5.6 Tree diagram for various attributes of risk evaluation

The stakeholder specific stream can be divided into the internal related and external related sub-streams. The first attribute of the internal-related sub-stream is goal and objective of the entity. Referring to the discussion in Chapter 4, Section 4.01, "risks do not exist without a reference to goals" (Wu, 2011). In risk evaluation for the decision on a risk response, a decision maker should always be reminded of the original (or ultimate) goals of the entity. For example, if a piece of used equipment is due for handover to an external buyer within months, there is no reason for the management to spend money on extending its insurance policy for more than a year. This goal and objective attribute is missing from most of the risk-management models, even though all researchers, as the author believes, are well aware of its importance.

Another internal related attribute is the resource and ability of the entity. No entity is able to provide unlimited resources for dealing with a particular risk item or category. Bubeck and colleagues (2012) use the term "response cost" to represent the "estimate of how costly it would be to actually implement the particular risk-reduction measures" (p. 1485). Referring to the findings of Siegrist and Gutscher (2008), the high cost of mitigation measures is one of the major reasons people do not take preventive measures for floods, even though they have experienced the risk beforehand (p. 775). Similarly for entities, a comparable example is the low percentage of companies that procure "loss of business" insurance mainly because of its high premium.

The ability of an entity mainly refers to the personnel talent within the organization. Although risk management is not uncommon, there are currently not too many companies that have designated risk-management departments, especially in small to medium-sized organizations. Even if a designated risk-management officer (or manager) is in place, he or she might not be competent enough to manage risk properly.

External related attributes of an entity include the perceived image (by external entities) and the subjective norm. Perceived image refers to how external stakeholders see the entity in terms of risk management. This is similar to "reputational risk" as per the classification of Whitfield (2003, p. 4). Referring to Section (b), a number of stakeholders are involved, but we will mainly focus on the image perceived by external customers. In the business world, the risk-taking attitude of an organization can affect the chance of gaining business. For example, a risk-averse customer may be less likely to do business with a high-risk-taking organization, and vice versa.

Subjective norm is derived from the TPB. In the risk-evaluation process, this can also be viewed as benchmarking to the industry common practice, even though the practice may not be the right or the most appropriate solution. For example, it is almost a common practice in the industry to have a redundant (dummy) computer server in a container terminal so that the IT system can switch between servers instantly when any of them is out of order.

The tree diagram as shown in Figure 5.6 identifies eight major attributes in risk evaluation, and the attributes related to stakeholder specific stream can be articulated to the stakeholders involved in the evaluation. Goal and objective is the main concern of the shareholders of an entity. Perceived image affects how the customer feels about the way the entity does business. Resource and ability relate to how and how much an organization can provide for dealing with a risk item, while subjective norm is the general practice the industry, mainly the competitors, follow when dealing with a particular risk item. Here, "competitor" is adopted instead of the whole industry mainly because (i) the industry may involve partners of the same group, and the way they handle risk may have been normalized already and (ii) the industry may involve other sectors such as companies of different scale serving different markets, and the way these companies handle risk may not be strictly comparable.

For the remaining four attributes, probability and severity relate to threat (risk), while cost and efficacy relate to the risk-reducing action (measure). By rearranging all eight attributes, a new model is developed, as shown in Figure 5.7. The model, the **Stakeholder Uniplanar Risk Evaluation** (SURE) model, starts with the risk item in the middle, with threat and action as the two major elements which are inter-related and mutually affecting each other. This is also the main reason for illustrating their relationship with a yin-yang icon.

This risk item in the middle is surrounded by four attributes, with probability and severity related to the threat (risk), while perceived cost and perceived efficacy relate to the risk-reducing action (measure). The four stakeholders to be taken into consideration for risk evaluation are shareholder, organization, customer and competitor, and their respective attributes are goal and objective, resource and ability, perceived image and subjective norm.

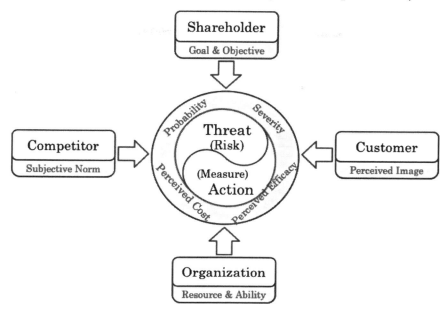

Figure 5.7 SURE model for risk evaluation

The term "uniplanar" is used because all these attributes and stakeholders are put together when reviewing the considerations for a risk decision, that is, in a single plane. Treating these attributes and stakeholders separately can result in missing the connections among them, and thus the decision on risk response might not take into account all aspects in relation to that particular risk item.

Based on the SURE model, it is interesting to see whether it can be effectively used in the management of operational risk in container terminals. The framework of the new model is shown in Figure 5.7.

If the risk-management process and other risk elements are further incorporated, the SURE model can be represented by Figure 5.8. Importantly, it focuses on how an individual working in a container terminal company makes risk-response decisions and how well the SURE model can be applied in the management of operational risk in container terminals. The derivation of the SURE model has been discussed in the previous chapter, and therefore it will not be repeated here.

Referring to the COSO ERM Framework, the SURE model concentrates only on three of the eight components in the model. These three components are event identification, risk assessment and risk response. Here, event identification can be considered the input for the model and risk response the output. The SURE model, as a result, can be considered the system for analysing the risk. One of the challenges of this research is figuring out how the elements in the input, output and system can be appropriately defined and applied to the container terminal industry.

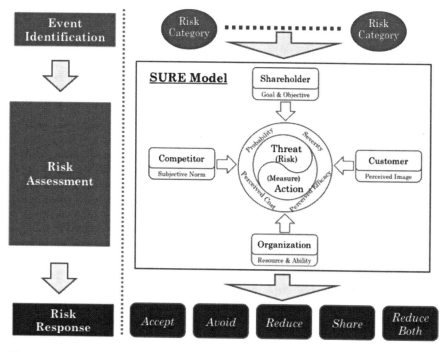

Figure 5.8 Conceptual framework of the current research

For event identification, it will be difficult for any research to carry out the study on all risk items unless these risk items are grouped into a few risk categories. Six different categories of risk have been identified by the author: natural disaster, accident caused by external event, accident caused by staff, breakdown/failure of equipment, breakdown/failure of it system and social and human issues. The description of each risk category has been discussed, and therefore it is not repeated here. However, this classification of risk categories might not be the most appropriate methodology to be applied in the container terminal industry. Here, the current study starts with some qualitative questions on this issue in order to verify the suitability of this classification.

For risk assessment, the current study makes use of the responses of the respondents to confirm that the eight attributes of the SURE model are a good representation of the factors that the decision makers consider. Because of the different background of the decision makers in terms of their location, size, shareholding structure, management composition and so on, these eight attributes might affect the decision makers differently. In this study, we also investigate the impact of various attributes based on the backgrounds of the decision makers and on different categories of risk.

Furthermore, this study also investigates the relationship between the eight attributes in the SURE model and the six risk categories. Based on different risk categories, decision makers pay different levels of attention to each of the risk attributes. This study also aims to reveal the relationships between them.

For risk response, the current study makes use of the Risk Node Coordinate concept described previously. The five strategies under this concept are accept, avoid, reduce, share and reduce both. This Risk Node Coordinate concept facilitates the current research in the sense that it provides a good platform for all respondents to quantify the risks before and after the risk item is addressed. With this concept in place, inherent risk and residual risk (Figure 5.3) are represented by a pair of coordinates – (S_1, P_1) and (S_2, P_2), respectively – and the differences in the coordinates are converted into the five strategies of risk response as per the previous discussion.

6 Application of the SURE model for risk management in container terminals

6.1 Background

In order to provide sufficient storage space for containers, the land area covered by a container terminal is usually on the order of tens of thousands of square meters. In the mainland, it is not uncommon to have a container terminal with land area exceeding 1 million square meters, such as the container terminals in Shanghai and Suzhou of China. This, in fact, is equivalent to the area of 150+ soccer fields.

The relatively huge area covered by a container terminal makes it practically impossible for the management to oversee every single corner and every single aspect at any given time, even when sophisticated CCTV and other monitoring systems are in place. As a result, the management in general has to rely on strategies, systems and tools for risk management.

Because of the mega scale of the land a container terminal covers, capital investment is comparatively huge in general. A single berth with quay length around 350 m, which is just sufficient for berthing of medium-size container vessels, may cost RMB 1 to 1.3 billion in China, inclusive of land price. In order to provide a reasonable service level to the customers, usually a container terminal consists of three to five berths, and therefore capital investment of a container terminal company, or a "container terminal project", is on the order of RMB 3 to 7 billion.

Container terminals involve plenty of people and equipment and usually occupy relatively large pieces of land, together with their associated water area. Risks, therefore, are almost everywhere. The Busan case mentioned earlier is one of the well-known cases in the industry. Recently a vessel collided with one of the container berths in Hong Kong and caused some damage to a container crane and broke one pile of the quay structure. The total cost for repair plus the cost of business interruption was close to $50 million! Another type of accident that commonly occurs in container terminals is the malpractice of the staff. For example, the falling of containers owing to being mis-positioned by the crane operator may cause serious damage to the containers and the vehicles below, and sometimes it may even cause fatalities as well.

Even if there is no catastrophic or fatal accident, frequent occurrence of minor accidents may result in penalty or temporary business-suspension orders being issued by the governing authorities, especially in Mainland China. Furthermore, a poor safety record may reduce the chance of being granted investment opportunities in the future or subsequent phases of a container port. This in turn introduces unnecessary competition within the same region, and the implication could be permanent.

The book would like to provide a handy tool to manage the operational risk of container terminals by comparing the current practices to the industry norm and identifying whether the SURE model is applicable in the risk-evaluation process. Furthermore, the relative importance of the attributes under the SURE model will provide terminal operators the strategic thinking on how to best manage their operational risks. With this in mind, it is possible to:

1. Identify the factors affecting the risk-response decision and develop a new risk-assessment model (SURE model) for managing operational risks in container terminals.
2. Assess the applicability of the newly developed SURE model in the operational risk management of container terminals in Hong Kong, China and other Asian countries.
3. Analyse how company characteristics affect the evaluation attributes in the SURE model, as well as their relative importance, which results in different risk-response decisions.
4. Identify and recommend the most effective operational risk-management methodology for container terminals.

6.2 Details of the SURE model in real application

The application of the SURE model is carried out by using a survey with questionnaire to obtain responses from professionals in the container terminal operations. The results provide insight into risk management in container terminal operations in the Asia-Pacific Region. Detailed use of the survey is discussed here, as companies and practitioners can make use of the model and the survey to make their own evaluation towards the risk management issues with their own scope of analysis.

(a) Focus of the application

The numerical representation of risk allows the idea to be analysed quantitatively. Since the data are numerical figures, it is easier to study the relationships among risk categories, attributes of the SURE model and risk responses. A number of hypotheses are set up in response to direct the application.

H1ij There is a relationship between company characteristics i towards the concerns over the risk attribute j (i: a: location [of the terminal], b: customer base, c: shareholding [structure], d: management [composition], e: terminal size; j: 1: probability, 2: severity, 3: perceived cost, 4: perceived efficacy, 5: goal and objective, 6: resource and ability, 7: perceived image, 8: subjective norm).

H2i There is an impact of risk attributes i on the risk response choice (i: 1: probability, 2: severity, 3: perceived cost, 4: perceived efficacy, 5: goal and objective, 6: resource and ability, 7: perceived image, 8: subjective norm).

H3i There is a relationship between concerns on risk attributes i and the risk categories (i: 1: probability, 2: severity, 3: perceived cost, 4: perceived efficacy, 5: goal and objective, 6: resource and ability, 7: perceived image, 8: subjective norm).

H4aj There is a relationship between concerns on risk attributes j and the reduction in risk probability (j: 1: probability, 2: severity, 3: perceived cost, 4: perceived efficacy, 5: goal and objectives, 6: resource and ability, 7: perceived image, 8: subjective norm).

H4b There is a relationship between concerns on risk response and the reduction in risk probability.

H4cj There is a relationship between concerns on company characteristics and the reduction in risk probability (j: 1: location [of the terminal], 2: customer base, 3: shareholding [structure], 4: management [composition], 5: terminal size, 6: risk category).

H5aj There is a relationship between concerns on risk attributes j and the reduction in risk severity (j: 1: probability, 2: severity, 3: perceived cost, 4: perceived efficacy, 5: goal and objective, 6: resource and ability, 7: perceived image, 8: subjective norm).

H5b There is a relationship between concerns on risk response and the reduction in risk severity.

H5cj There is a relationship between concerns on company characteristic j and the reduction in risk severity (j: 1: location [of the terminal], 2: customer base, 3: shareholding [structure], 4: management [composition], 5: terminal size, 6: risk category).

Two observation analyses without hypotheses are also carried out in this application. These two analyses aim to find out (1) the relationship pattern between the risk-response preference (use of external help and number of responses used) with the company characteristics and (2) the relationship pattern between risk response and the risk items.

With this comprehensive list of analyses being carried out, all elements in the risk evaluation are investigated thoroughly, and this provides a clear picture of the application of the SURE model in the operational risk management of container terminals.

(b) Data collection method and measuring method

The survey is carried out by using well-structured questionnaires. As the risk-management strategies adopted by a container terminal may not be well understood by all levels of employees within the organization, this study focuses on management staff who really possess the insights.

This survey examines how container terminals respond to operational risk categories. Except for the extremely autocratic style of management, the decision on how to respond to an operational risk is usually made collectively by the management team. As a result, the data collected from this research reflect the decision of the organization, even though they are collected from individuals (Yin, 2009, p. 88). Therefore, the unit of analysis is the organization – the container terminal company.

The individual representing a container terminal company shall either be the general manager, operations manager, engineering manager or safety/risk manager. Individuals having positions other than these four are assessed on a case-by-case basis, and the main criterion for accepting that individual as a research participant is that the individual being invited to take the survey has full understanding of the risk-management strategy of the company.

Since the unit of analysis is the container terminal company, the gender of the respondent is not a critical issue in the analysis. Furthermore, the container terminal industry, in particular operational management, is dominated by males, and therefore it may not be easy to obtain sufficient response from females for this study.

As the time of senior managers is valuable and the locations of the terminals are spread over almost the entire Asian continent, it is not possible to carry out a face-to-face interview with each participant. The current study therefore relies on the self-administered questionnaire to obtain the responses. The pragmatism allows almost all types of data collection methods. The following sections detail how the questionnaire is designed in order to increase its completeness and the justification of the sample used in this study.

The questionnaire adopted in this survey is shown in Appendix 1, with Part A being the qualitative questions, Part B being the quantitative questions and Part C being the questions asking for the background of the respondents and his/her container terminal company.

(c) Details of the questionnaire filling and its responses

For each risk category, the participants were asked to quantify it by making reference to the scales as shown in Table 6.2. The risk before (inherent risk) and after (residual risk) risk response and treatment are represented by a pair of nodes with two-dimensional coordinates (S, P). The differences in risk coordinates between inherent and residual risks reveal what risk-response strategy the participant has taken for that particular risk category.

In the second part of the questionnaire, the participants were asked about the relative importance of each of the eight attributes they had considered before the risk-response decision was made. The relative importance was to be reflected by using the scale from 1 to 7, with 1 being "not relevant" and 7 being "extremely important". By summarizing the results of "relative importance" for each attribute, together with the analysis of the background of the participants, the major causes and the major attributes in different risk responses were revealed.

In the last part of the questionnaire, the participants were asked to complete a number of questions regarding the characteristics of the company they were working with (details are discussed in the later part of this chapter). All three parts were used for quantitative analysis of this study.

(d) Sample size in the application

Based on some unconfirmed statistics, the total number of sizeable container terminal companies in Asia exceeds 300. The goal of the survey was to receive responses from at least 30 container terminal companies, and this survey covers various locations of major container terminals in East and Southeast Asia, except for terminals in Japan, Taiwan, India, Malaysia and Thailand. During the course of the survey questionnaire, management of the left-out container terminal companies could not be reached or contacted, and therefore they were skipped.

In this study, 32 replies from various container terminal companies were received. However, since two of the replies were incomplete, ultimately 30 questionnaire responses were used for the quantitative analysis.

Distribution of the respondents is encouraging. Table 6.1 shows the rankings of the world's top 50 container port in 2012 (and also 2011) based on container

Table 6.1 Ports' ranking in 2012 and their participation in this research

Rank	Port, Country	Volume (Mil TEUs)		Participated in this survey
		2012	*2011*	
1	Shanghai, China	32.53	31.74	✓
2	Singapore, Singapore	31.65	29.94	✓
3	Hong Kong, China	23.10	24.38	✓
4	Shenzhen, China	22.94	22.57	✓
5	Busan, South Korea	17.04	16.18	✓
6	Ningbo-Zhoushan, China	16.83	14.72	✓
7	Guangzhou, China	14.74	14.42	✓
8	Qingdao, China	14.50	13.02	✓
9	Jebel Ali, Dubai, UAE	13.30	13.00	
10	Tianjin, China	12.30	11.59	✓
11	Rotterdam, Netherlands	11.87	11.88	
12	Port Kelang, Malaysia	10.00	9.60	
13	Kaohsiung, Taiwan, China	9.78	9.64	
14	Hamburg, Germany	8.86	9.01	
15	Antwerp, Belgium	8.64	8.66	
16	Los Angeles, United States	8.08	7.94	
17	Dalian, China	8.06	6.40	
18	Keihin ports*, Japan	7.85	7.64	

Rank	Port, Country	Volume (Mil TEUs) 2012	Volume (Mil TEUs) 2011	Participated in this survey
19	Tanjung Pelepas, Malaysia	7.70	7.50	
20	Xiamen, China	7.20	6.47	✓
21	Bremen, Germany	6.12	5.92	
22	Tanjung Priok, Indonesia	6.10	5.62	✓
23	Long Beach, United States	6.05	6.06	
24	Laem Chabang, Thailand	5.93	5.73	
25	New York-New Jersey, United States	5.53	5.50	
26	Ho Chi Minh, Vietnam	5.19	4.53	✓
27	Lianyungang, China	5.02	4.85	
28	Hanshin* ports, Japan	5.00	4.80	
29	Yingkou, China	4.85	4.03	
30	Jeddah, Saudi Arabia	4.74	4.01	
31	Valencia, Spain	4.47	4.33	
32	Colombo, Sri Lanka	4.26	4.26	✓
33	Jawaharlal Nehru, India	4.26	4.32	
34	Algeciras Bay, Spain	4.07	3.60	
35	Sharjah, UAE	4.00	3.23	✓
36	Felixstowe, U.K.	3.95	3.74	
37	Port Said, Egypt	3.91	3.91	
38	Manila, Philippines	3.71	3.46	
39	Salalah, Oman	3.63	3.20	
40	Colon, Panama	3.52	3.37	
41	Balboa, Panama	3.30	3.23	
42	Santos, Brazil	3.17	2.99	
43	Ambarli, Turkey	3.10	2.69	
44	Georgia Ports, United States	2.97	2.94	
45	Nagoya, Japan	2.87	2.62	
46	Tanjung Perak, Indonesia	2.85	2.64	
47	Gioia Tauro, Italy	2.72	2.30	
48	Metro Vancouver, Canada	2.71	2.51	
49	Melbourne, Australia	2.60	2.51	
50	Durban, South Africa	2.59	2.71	

*Keihin Ports is Japan's superport hub on the Tokyo Bay and includes Yokohama, Kawasaki and Tokyo. Hanshin Ports is Japan's superport hub on the Osaka Bay and includes Kobe, Osaka, Sakai-Semboku and Amagasaki-Nishinomiya-Ashiya

Source: *The Journal of Commerce*, August 20, 2012, and August 19, 2013

Note: Represents total port throughput, including loaded and empty TEU.

throughput. Within the top 10 ports in the list, 9 of them had container terminal companies that participated in this survey, which accounts for 90% of the top 10 ports.

On the other hand, there are 20 ports among the top 50 that were not in Asia in 2012. If these non-Asian ports are not considered, there are 30 Asian ports in the top 50. Within these 30 Asian top 50 ports, this study received replies from 14 ports (47%), all of them within the top 40. And if only the top 40 ports are taken into calculation, there are 28 Asian ports, and the percentage of participation is equal to 50% (14/28). With this high coverage of major ports, the result provides a very insightful view of risk management of container terminals in Asia.

As mentioned previously, the capital investment of a container terminal is huge. In order to share the risk and to incorporate strategic partners such as shipping companies, it is not uncommon for a container terminal company to have more than one shareholder. This is one of the main reasons for the high percentage (53%) of joint-venture companies among those that participated in this survey.

6.3 Measurement and operationalization

The variables in the model are the eight attributes as discussed in 5.02(c) above (see also Figure 5.6). These eight attributes – probability, severity, perceived cost, perceived efficacy, goal and objective, resource and ability, perceived image and subjective norm – are used to identify whether the SURE model can be appropriately adopted in risk evaluation process.

Referring to the typical risk matrix (Figure 5.2) and the discussions in Section 5.01(d), a qualitative approach is used to justify the SURE model. For the application of the model and its impact on risk management, a quantitative approach is used. Following are detailed explanations of the measurement of variables in this application.

Risk category is measured by using the Risk Node Coordinate concept, both the inherent and the residual. The scale of the two axes of risk matrix is shown in Table 6.2. Severity of a risk item can be measured in a few dimensions, such as the

Table 6.2 Scales of the two axes in risk matrix

Actual Probability	$P =$	Actual Severity (in HKD)	$S =$
$P < 0.00001\%$	1	$S < 100$	1
$0.00001\% \leq P < 0.0001\%$	2	$100 \leq S < 1,000$	2
$0.0001\% \leq P < 0.001\%$	3	$1,000 \leq S < 10,000$	3
$0.001\% \leq P < 0.01\%$	4	$10,000 \leq S < 100,000$	4
$0.01\% \leq P < 0.1\%$	5	$100,000 \leq S < 1\ \text{Mil}$	5
$0.1\% \leq P < 1\%$	6	$1\ \text{Mil} \leq S < 10\ \text{Mil}$	6
$1\% \leq P < 10\%$	7	$10\ \text{Mil} \leq S < 100\ \text{Mil}$	7
$10\% \leq P < 100\%$	8	$100\ \text{Mil} \leq S$	8

number of fatalities. In general, the most common dimension used in risk analysis is still loss in monetary terms. The monetary value mentioned here includes all direct and indirect costs and/or loss induced by the respective risk category when it does happen.

For probability, the percentage as shown in Table 6.2 means the chance of occurrence. However, this "chance of occurrence" is a time-related measurement. For example, the chance of an earthquake within one year will be substantially lower than the chance of its occurrence within a hundred years. In order to provide a common ground for analysis, we have assumed a 5-year period in the estimation of chance of occurrence, mainly because normally an insurance policy will not cover a period longer than 5 years. The participants' replies referring to Table 6.2 not only show the actual status of the risk category but also help the company to identify its effectiveness in reducing the subsequent impact as well as identifying the responses that are used by the company in tackling such events.

According to the definitions of various risk responses, the "reduce both" option can be represented by a reduction in the scales in both probability and severity. If only reduction in the scale of probability is found, it is equivalent to the use of the "reduce" risk response. On the other hand, sole reduction of the severity scale is equivalent to the use of "share" risk response, and no change in the scale is equivalent to the use of "acceptance" risk response. "Avoid" is rarely adopted by the respondents of this study, as it would have been difficult for the respondents to recall any risk category that has happened in the past but is now eliminated artificially (such as the abandoning of containers carrying explosives). These "avoided" risks are easily ignored by the decision makers once they do not exist anymore, and thus they are not reflected or reported.

Six categories of risk have been identified as per the discussion in Section 4.02, and the detailed descriptions for each of them are summarized in Table 6.3. In order to confirm that these six risk categories included all major operational risks in container terminals, the decision makers were asked to provide additional category(s) of operational risk, if any.

Classification of the diversity (characteristics) of container terminal companies being studied is shown in Table 6.4. The companies that participated in this study are classified according to their location, business nature, shareholding structure,

Table 6.3 Summary of risk categories in this study

Category	Descriptions
A	Natural Disaster (typhoon, tsunami, earthquake, etc.)
B	Accidents caused by External Events (ship colliding quay, terrorists, etc.)
C	Accidents caused by Staff (carelessness, misconduct, etc.)
D	Breakdown/failure of Equipment (design fault, material fatigue, etc.)
E	Breakdown/failure of IT System (breakdown, hacker, etc.)
F	Social and Human Issues (labour strike, etc.)

Table 6.4 Diversity of container terminal companies to be surveyed

Categories	Sub-categories	Descriptions
By Location	Hong Kong	
	China	Mainland China except HK
	S.E. Asia	
	Others	
By Biz Nature (Customer)	Domestic	> 50% container throughput in domestic trade
	International	> 50% container T/P in international trade
By Shareholding	State-Owned	Dominantly owned by state-owned enterprises
	Joint Venture	Dominantly owned by foreign investors
	Private Entity	Dominantly owned by local private companies
By Management	Full International	> 3 senior managers are expatriates (incl. HK)
	Semi-international	1 to 2 senior managers are expatriates (incl. HK)
	Local	All senior managers are locals
By Terminal Size	> 70,000 DWT	Capable of berthing > 70,000 DWT vessel
	10 ~ 70K DWT	Capable of berthing 10,000 ~ 70,000 DWT vessel
	< 10,000 DWT	Capable of berthing < 10,000 DWT vessel only

management structure and terminal size. Details of the classification, together with the descriptions for each category and sub-category, are stated in Table 6.4.

With this classification in place, these variables are used for analysing their relationships with the evaluation attributes and with the risk-response decisions.

6.4 Data analysis techniques

To complete the data analysis, a number of methods are used in this study. For the qualitative part, content analysis is used, in particular for replies to the open-ended questions. For the quantitative part, ANOVA and independent t-test, multinomial regression analysis, logistic regression and correspondence analysis are used.

(a) Content analysis

Content analysis is a method to analyse written, audio or visual messages (Cole, 1988). It was first used to analyse hymns, newspapers, magazines, advertisement and political speeches (Harwood and Garry, 2003). Currently, it is widely used in psychology, business and other contexts. Holsti (1969) had grouped the 15 uses of content analysis into three main categories: (i) make inferences about the antecedents of a communication, (ii) describe and make inferences about characteristics of a communication and, (iii) make inferences about the effects of a communication.

Among these three categories, the application falls into the second category for justifying the need to carry out the content analysis. The study aims to "compare communication content to standards". The responses (communication content) provided by the respondents on risk attributes, risk items and other related information can be compared with the predefined attributes and items in the SURE model (standard), which are derived from the modification and consolidation of two very traditional and well-known theories. Moreover, it also justifies whether the necessary and relevant elements have been included.

(b) Analysis of variance (ANOVA) and independent t-test

Analysis of variance (ANOVA) is used to compare the differences in mean scores of various predefined groups. In the current study, the characteristics of the container terminal companies are consolidated, based on their different backgrounds, into a number of predefined groups. The mean scores in the attributes are compared in order to find out whether the specific nature/characteristics of the company would lead to a difference in the concerns over the risk attributes. This is to analyse the risk attributes demographically. As most of the characteristics variables consist of three or more categories, ANOVA therefore is the most appropriate method. However, for the group under Customer Base, there are only two sub-groups of note. Here, to observe the limitation of the analysing methodology, an independent t-test is used instead of ANOVA. As a result, these two methods, ANOVA and independent t-test, are used for testing hypotheses (H1ij) and (H3i).

(c) Logistic regression

Different from the ordinary regression analysis, logistic regression makes predictions for dichotomous data. That means the outcome variables can only take one of the two possible values predefined. One of the major concerns of logistic regression is to find out the probability or likelihood of having a particular outcome. The logistic function can be represented by the following formula:

$$\ln\left(\frac{\hat{p}}{1-\hat{p}}\right) = \beta_0 + \beta_1 x_1 + \beta_2 x_2 + \beta_3 x_3 + \dots + \beta_m x_m$$

$\hat{p}$ for a given value of x can be obtained by:

$$\hat{p} = \frac{\exp\left(\beta_0 + \beta_1 x_1 + \beta_2 x_2 + \beta_3 x_3 + \dots + \beta_m x_m\right)}{1 + \exp\left(\beta_0 + \beta_1 x_1 + \beta_2 x_2 + \beta_3 x_{13} + \dots + \beta_m x_m\right)}$$

$$\frac{e^{\beta_0 + \beta_1 x_1 + \beta_2 x_2 + \beta_3 x_3 + \ldots + \beta_m x_m}}{1 + e^{\beta_0 + \beta_1 x_1 + \beta_2 x_2 + \beta_3 x_{13} + \ldots + \beta_m x_m}}$$

Since $\hat{p}$ represents the probability that $Y = 1$, $1 - \hat{p}$ represents the probability that $Y = 0$.ln is natural logarithm and the right-hand side is the normal regression line. β_0 represents the intercept, other $\beta_1, \beta_2, \beta_3 \ldots$ represent the regression coefficient and x_1, x_2, x_3 are the values of the independent variables. Such natural logarithm operation is needed because the right-hand side of the formula will have input value from negative infinity to positive infinity, while the $\hat{p}$ and $1 - \hat{p}$ can only take the values between 0 and 1, as they are representing the probabilities.

Generally speaking, a positive value of the regression coefficient means that the increase in the corresponding x would lead to an increase in the probability of that outcome. As we are examining the likelihood of $Y = 1$ (with probability of $\hat{p}$), the positive value of the coefficient represents that an increase in X would cause an increase in the probability of having $Y = 1$. Furthermore, the relationship between the independent variables and the binary outcome can be easily obtained through logistic regression.

H4 and H5 investigate the impact of various attributes, company characteristics, risk categories and risk responses on the effectiveness of the reduction of probability and severity. As the dependent variables are transformed into binary values, therefore, the use of logistic regression would be more appropriate.

(d) Multinomial logistic regression

The multinomial logistic regression model is a classification model which generalizes the traditional logistic regression model to multiclass problems. Basically, it predicts the probabilities of different possible outcomes for the categorical dependent variable with more than two classes (Greene, 1993, p. 720–723), or referred to as "polytomous" cases. The independent variables can be either continuous or categorical. This method makes use of the linear predictor function to predict the probability of observation i having the outcome j with the following formula:

$$f(k,i) = \beta_{0,j} + \beta_{1,j} x_{1,i} + \beta_{2,j} x_{2,i} + \ldots + \beta_{k,j} x_{k,i}$$

where $\beta_{k,j}$ is a regression coefficient for kth variable and jth outcome. $\beta_{0,j}$ is the intercept and $x_{k,i}$ is the value of the observation i for variable k.

The process of the multinomial logistic regression can be regarded as running $j - 1$ binary logistic regression when there are altogether j possible outcomes. One outcome would be chosen as the pivot, and the remaining $j - 1$ outcomes would be regressed individually against the pivot. For example, when outcome j is chosen as the pivot:

$$ln\frac{Pr\left(Y_i=1\right)}{Pr\left(Y_i=j\right)}=\beta_1.X_i\ldots\ldots ln\frac{Pr\left(Y_i=j-1\right)}{Pr\left(Y_i=j\right)}=\beta_{j-1}.X_i$$

where the right-hand side for each formula is a vector size $k+1$ (k independent variables).

By applying exponentiation to both sides of each formula and by making use of the idea that the outcome must fall into any one of the outcomes and thus the total probability adds up to 1, the probability for having the *j*th outcome would be:

$$\Pr\left(Y_i=j\right)=\frac{1}{1+\sum_{j=1}^{j-1}e^{\beta_j.x_i}}$$

and the probability for other outcomes can be derived from:

$$\Pr\left(Y_i=1\right)=\frac{e^{\beta_1 x_i}}{1+\sum_{j=1}^{j-1}e^{\beta_j x_i}}\ldots\ldots\Pr\left(Y_i=j-1\right)=\frac{e^{\beta_{j-1} x_i}}{1+\sum_{j=1}^{j-1}e^{\beta_j x_i}}$$

H2 has responses limited to a number of outcomes (more than two) in which they are mutually exclusive. The use of multinomial logistic regression is justifiable for identifying how the risk attributes would affect the probability or likelihood in choosing a specific risk response (reduce, reduce both, share, accept) and, in this case, for handling different risk categories in container terminal operations.

(e) Multiple correspondence analysis (MCA)

Multiple correspondence analysis (MCA) has been widely used in market research studies to facilitate the association between the demographic variables under investigation and the behaviour variables. For example, Hoffman and Batra (1991) made use of MCA to show the association between TV program types and viewing behaviours. Sometimes MCA is treated as a graphical representation of the variables, which can also be displayed in matrix format. The usage interchange between matrix and graph (correspondence analysis, or CA) is easy when only two variables are under investigation. However, when there are more than two variables, MCA, which reduces the dimensions and puts the object and category in a plot, provides a good solution for such analysis. CA, therefore, is considered a special case under MCA when only two variables are being analysed (Hoffman and Leeuw, 1992).

Basically, the point location and the closeness are used for analysing MCA graphs (joint plot, object plot and category plot). The closeness of the points demonstrates a possibly stronger relationship between the categories and/or the objects. The point location represents the frequency of the category or object.

For example, low marginal frequency is represented by a point located at the edge of the plot, while a high marginal frequency will be presented by a point around the original.

Other than the hypotheses, some tasks are carried out in order to find out the association between the demographic variables of companies (company characteristics) and the risk treatments (1. number of responses and use of external help with company's demography; 2. risk category and risk response). As the variables in these tasks are categorical in nature and the number of variables is larger than two, MCA and CA are used for such analyses.

7 Findings of the application of the SURE model for risk management in container terminals

7.1 Findings from the qualitative analysis

(a) Verification of risk attributes in SURE model

The proposed SURE model intends to include eight attributes: 1: probability, 2: severity, 3: perceived cost, 4: perceived efficacy, 5: goal and objectives, 6: resource and ability, 7: perceived image and 8: subjective norm. To justify the inclusion of these elements and thus the SURE model, opinions were obtained from various container terminal companies in Asia. Questionnaires covering both qualitative and quantitative issues were sent to the senior managers of the terminals. The respondents to these questionnaires included operations managers, general managers of the operation and chief operation officers who are familiar with container terminal operations.

In order to analyse the qualitative data, content analysis was carried out following Elo and Kyngas (2007). This application focuses on justifying the appropriateness of the predefined elements, and thus the deductive approach content analysis described by Elo and Kyngas should be used (see Table 7.1).

The eight attributes of the SURE model are discussed in Section 5.02, but the detailed target wordings or ideas need to be defined. The SURE model intends to look at the attributes with the descriptions summarized in Table 7.2.

(b) Selecting risk-response decision

Question 5 of the questionnaire is chosen for analysis, as the limitations are often related to the concerns that come up in the decision makers' minds when dealing with the risks. All responses are quoted and summarized directly if related ideas and wordings are identified. The key words are highlighted in Table 7.3.

From the analysis, the following observations are identified:

(i)   Probability is not mentioned directly by the respondents. There are responses like the "inability to control the risk event", which are indirectly related to the occurrence of risk events. However, with the traditional ideas mentioned in the literature review chapter (Section 4.01(b)), this element

Table 7.1 Steps for content analysis in supporting the SURE model

Selecting the unit of analysis	Responses to the question "What are the limitations that affect your company in selecting the most suitable risk treatment method?"
Making sense of the data and the whole	All the responses received are used and read carefully several times and retyped into the computer so as to get analysts familiar with the content.
Developing structured analysis matrix	The matrices are developed already with the eight elements.
Data coding according to the categories	Choose only aspects that fit the category.
Hypothesis testing, correspondence comparison to earlier studies – trustworthiness	As the SURE model is a newly proposed model, the trustworthiness is verified by cross-checking the answers with the respondents and seeking opinions from other professionals.
Reporting the analysing process and the results	The elements supporting each risk attribute are listed in the tables in the following sections.

Table 7.2 Detailed explanation on the structured category for content analysis

Evaluation Attributes	Description
Probability	The probability of a risk before risk treatment
Severity	The severity of a risk before risk treatment
Perceived Cost	Estimated cost (both direct and indirect) of risk treatment method
Perceived Efficacy	Anticipated effectiveness of the risk treatment method
Goal and Objective	Business goal and objective of the container terminal company
Resource and Ability	How and how much a company can provide to deal with a risk
Perceived Image	How the customers feel about the way the company handles risk
Subjective Norm	The general practice the industry takes in dealing with a risk

is often involved in risk-related evaluation issues, and thus it should be included in the SURE model even though it is not particularly mentioned by the respondents.

(ii) Severity and cost are the two attributes in which direct wordings can be identified.

(iii) There are quite a number of responses referring to the cost element.
(iv) Effectiveness is classified as the perceived efficacy, as the definition for this attribute is the anticipated effectiveness of the risk treatment. Feasibility tests mentioned by the respondents also include the impact and the expected results of the risk-response decision, and thus it should be treated as perceived efficacy.
(v) Parent company strategies are often treated as the guidelines for operations, and they may be turned into the goal and objective.
(vi) Input and output, as well as manpower, are the resources of the company, while knowledge towards the risk events should be regarded as ability.
(vii) Customer expectations, reputation and business impact are all related to the perception towards the company and thus should be treated as the perceived image.
(viii) Industry norm is the common industry practice and should be put under the subjective norm.

There are other responses (part of the responses in Table 7.3) that have not been consolidated in the summary, as they do not fit into any of the evaluation attributes. However, they are not further classified into other risk attributes in the SURE model. Table 7.4 summarizes the reasons these responses are not included in the eight attributes, and it also lists the reasons for not opening up new risk attributes. With these arguments in place, it confirms that the eight attributes in the SURE model can in generally embrace all concerns of the decision makers in the operational risk management of container terminal companies.

(c) *Validity of six predefined categories of operational risk*

Referring to Figure 5.8, the INPUT of this study is Event Identification. Referring to 4.02, six risk categories were predefined by the author for use in this analysis.

During the questionnaire survey, the respondents were asked in the first place the validity of these predefined risk categories, and the question is as follows:

"Q1. Other than these 6 categories of risk, any other risk categories you consider important in the operational risk management of your company?"

Seventy per cent of the respondents replied that the six categories so defined covered all operational risks encountered by container terminals. The remaining 30% of the respondents mentioned a few risk items and considered them "other risk categories". However, based on detailed analysis of these "other risk items", they can actually be fitted into the predefined risk categories of this study easily. Details of the categorization are shown in Table 7.5. As a result, there is no need to have any additional risk category to this study, and the six risk categories predefined previously provided a solid foundation for the subsequent research.

Table 7.3 Content analysis with responses grouped by risk attributes

Evaluation Attributes	Responses to the question "What are the limitations that affect your company in selecting the most suitable risk treatment method?"
Probability	• Inability to control risk events like natural disasters
Severity	• According to the risk event time, place, category, impact area, *severity*, following events
Perceived Cost	• Financial *cost* control;
	• Local regulations and *cost* are the factors that need to be concerned;
	• Safety, law, *cost* (including insurance);
	• *Cost* incurred and the knowledge towards the risk;
	• Concept and *cost*;
	• *Cost* and Effectiveness
	• Terminal operations constraints, *financial* and manpower resources
Perceived Efficacy	• Cost and *effectiveness*
	• Government and *industry norm*, input and output, impact on terminal operation and *feasibility test*
Goal and Objective	• *Matching between parent company's* (major shareholders or shareholders) *strategies* and the real situation
Resource and Ability	• Government and industry norm, *input and output*, impact on terminal operation and feasibility test
	• *Insufficient experience, knowledge and manpower*
	• Terminal operation constraints, *financial and manpower resources*
	• Cost incurred and the *knowledge towards the risk*;
	• *Capital, time*
Perceived Image	• Risk score, legal compliance, *business impact*, etc.
	• Government and/or *customer expectation*
	• Risk category, customer service, *reputation*
Subjective Norm	• Government and *industry norm*, input and output, impact on terminal operation and feasibility test
	• The local government departments; the current *preparedness of adjacent terminal operators* and working parties on business continuity management

(d) Standard procedures in risk treatment

Question 2 focuses on the standard procedures of risk treatment, and the respondents were asked:

"Q2. Is there any standard procedure(s) in your company for selecting the risk treatment method for different categories of risk?"

Table 7.4 Justifications for not categorizing other replies as additional risk attributes

Replies from Respondents	Reasons for not categorized as Attribute
• According to the *risk event time, place, category*, impact area, severity, *following events*	(i) The response is likely to vary. Places of occurrence may be too broad for analysis.
• *Risk category,* customer service, reputation	(ii) Following event is already included in the risk response and outside the focus of the risk attributes.
	(iii) Risk category has been analysed as a grouping of variables rather than an independent variable.
• Law, administrative rules/regulations	(i) These risks shall be covered under the "Compliance Risk" instead of "Operational Risk" as defined in COSO ERM Framework.
• *Risk score, legal compliance,* business impact, etc.	
• Host country rules, regulations and policies	
• *Local regulations* and cost are the factors that need to be concerned;	
• *Safety, law,* cost (including insurance)	
• Government	(i) The responses that highlighted the impact of the government are very location specific and focus on the container terminal at a particular location.
• *The local government departments,* the current preparedness of adjacent terminal operators and working parties on business continuity management	(ii) It also relates to the "Compliance Risk" in the risk management.
• *Government* and industry norm, input and output, impact on terminal operation and feasibility test	
• *Government* and/or customer expectation	
• External parties such as labour union, government directives and political influence	
• Location setting and environment throughout; equipment status	(i) These shall be treated as the company background rather than the risk attributes.
• *Facility,* equipment	
• Accuracy in prediction	(i) These are indirect to the efficacy and not comprehensive enough to constitute a category.
• Valuation on external threat	

Table 7.5 Categorizing "other risk items" into predefined risk categories

Predefined categories that can be classified	A. Natural Disaster	B. Accident caused by External Event	C. Accident caused by Staff	D. Equipment Breakdown	E. IT System Breakdown	F. Social & Human Issues	Remarks
Injury, Diseases			✓			✓	
Diseases, Pollution and Block on Routes						✓	
Blackout, Food Poisoning						✓	
Explosive, chemical and radiation leakage from cargo inside container; Handling of DG containers		✓					
Fraud Risk (e.g. Asset Misappropriation, Fraudulent Statements, Corruption)			✓				[Compliance Risk]
Car accidents by external parties		✓					
Change in shareholding; change in political parties/Government parties; relationship w. landlord							Not Operational Risk
Contractor						✓	

Referring to replies of the respondents, there are a number of standard procedures for handling risks. Table 7.6 summarizes the standard procedures mentioned by the respondents, and these standard procedures are classified based on the six predefined risk categories of this study.

Table 7.6 Standard procedures for selecting risk treatment method

Category	Details
Natural Disaster	Procedures for road safety under bad weather
	Procedures for handling natural disasters
	Procedures for operations under typhoon
	Procedures for operations under tidal waves and flooding
	Prevention of water pollution
Accident caused by External Event	Fire emergency plan
	Procedures for handling damaged goods
	Procedures for handling dangerous goods
	Procedures for handling car accidents
	Procedures for handling port safety
	Procedures for handling shipwreck
	Emergency communication plan
	Reporting procedures for uncontrollable events
	Virus response procedures
Accident caused by Staff	Procedures for handling on-site accidents
	Safety management handbook
	Key performance index for staff
Breakdown/failure of Equipment	Procedures for handling special equipment
	Procedures for handling equipment breakdown
	Procedures for handling equipment under windy conditions
	Container operations process control procedures
	Equipment management procedures
	Safety regulations and procedures
Breakdown/failure of IT System	Computers and network control procedures
	Procedures for handling system blackout and power off
	Information system security framework
Social and Human Issue (labour strike, etc.)	Contingency plans for public health emergencies
	Procedures for handling food poisoning
	Customer handling standard
	Appraisal system
Overall	Special operation procedures

Table 7.7 Internal parties involved in risk treatment decision

People	Department
Senior management	Safety and Security
Shareholders	Engineering
General manager	Operations
Director	Financial
Risk-handling committee	IT
Duty manager	Risk
Relevant staff in the risk events	Human resources
	Commercial

Table 7.8 Measurement of risk treatment method effectiveness

Category	Details
Breakdown/failure of Equipment	• Equipment Key Performance Index • Equipment status check • Yard status check
Breakdown/failure of IT System	• Web Key Performance Index
Overall	• Regular emergency drills • Touch and call • Occurrence • Money loss • Financial and time impact on business interruption • Risk level • Auditing • Regulations and measurements borrow from the other operators • Training rate • Safety targets • Contrast on the figures before and after risk treatment

(e) Internal parties involved in risk treatment decision

Question 4 requested the respondents to reveal the internal parties involved in risk treatment decisions, and the question is:

"Q4. Which party/parties will be involved in selecting the risk treatment method for operational risk of your company?"

Table 7.7 summarizes the parties involved in selecting the risk treatment method for operational risk.

Table 7.9 Responses to other questions in qualitative part of questionnaire

Questions	Replies obtained from Respondents
Q3. Time required for making risk-handling decision	More than 70% of the companies can make the decision within days.
Q7. Communicate with external parties before selecting the risk responses	87% of the companies have communicated with external parties before selecting the risk responses, and these external parties include: • Insurers • Authorities, government bodies • Other port companies • Solicitors • Customers • Consultant
Q8. Knowledge on the risk treatment methods used in the industry	All respondents revealed that they have knowledge of industry practice, but the knowledge does not extend to all risk categories.
Q9. Impact of goal and objective on risk response decision	More than 50% of the respondents said that there are some impacts for goals and objectives on risk-response decisions, but the impacts do not apply to all risk categories. Others think that their risk decisions are in line with the goals and objectives.
Q10. Impact of perceived image on risk-response decision	45% and 39% of the responses, respectively, revealed that they will consider or will partially consider the company image in all risk treatment method decisions. The remaining 16% replied that they will not consider the company image at all when they make risk-response decisions.

(f) Measuring the effectiveness of risk treatment method

Question 6 focuses on the efficacy of the risk response, and the question is:

"Q6. How does your company measure the effectiveness of your risk treatment methods?"

Unlike the standard procedures, the measurement of risk treatment method's effectiveness is companywide rather than risk category specific or department specific. Table 7.8 summarizes the measurement methods mentioned by the respondents.

(g) Responses to other qualitative questions

For other questions in the qualitative part of the questionnaire, Table 7.9 summarizes the results obtained from the respondents. These results are useful in demonstrating some key ideas in the risk management of container terminal operations, and their implications are discussed in Chapter 8.

7.2 Findings from the quantitative analysis

(a) Demographic distribution of the respondents

Prior to detailed analysis of quantitative questions, the characteristics of the companies that the respondents are working with are examined. Figure 7.1 shows the distribution of locations of the terminals that participated in this survey.

In this survey, more than half of the participants come from container terminal companies in Mainland China. Of the top 10 ports in the world in terms of container throughput, 6 ports (excluding Hong Kong) are in Mainland China. For the remaining participants, ports from Hong Kong, Southeast Asia and others basically have equal shares. As such, the representation of this survey shall in general be valid to cover the area this study intends to investigate.

Figure 7.2 shows the distribution of customer base of the container terminal companies that participated in this survey. In general, container terminal companies can charge a higher tariff for global traffic, compared to domestic destinations, mainly because there are more procedural formalities involved in the case of international destinations such as customs clearance. Moreover, container terminals serving domestic customers are usually smaller in size. As discussed in the previous chapters, they are not the main targets for this analysis, but the incorporation of this type of terminal will provide a better comparison and understanding to the industry as a whole.

In this study, distributions of company characteristics including shareholding structure, management composition and terminal size are shown in Figure 7.3, Figure 7.4 and Figure 7.5, respectively. These diagrams provide an overview of these characteristics, and their respective findings are discussed in the following chapters.

(b) Company characteristics and risk attributes

To view the differences in concerns of risk attributes, H1ij (i: a: location, b: customer base, c: shareholding, d: management, e: size; j: 1: probability, 2: severity,

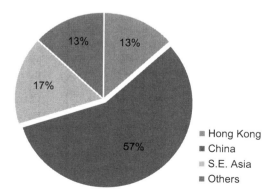

Figure 7.1 Locations of terminals in this research

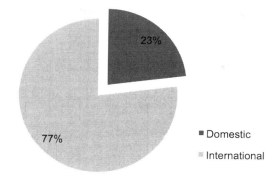

Figure 7.2 Customer base of terminals in this research

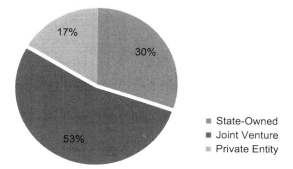

Figure 7.3 Shareholding structure of terminals in this research

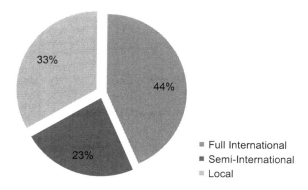

Figure 7.4 Management composition of terminals in this research

3: perceived cost, 4: perceived efficacy, 5: goal and objectives, 6: resource and ability, 7: perceived image, 8: subjective norm) was tested with ANOVA (*t-test is used for the customer base, as there are only two groups, international and domestic), and the average attribute scores were used. Significance is set at 0.05,

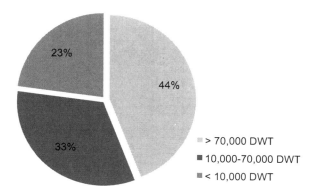

Figure 7.5 Size of terminals in this research

which means that a difference in attribute concerns is present when the *p*-value is less than 0.05. In other words, the specific company background is likely to affect the risk attribute concerned when the H1ij is rejected. For hypotheses that are rejected, post-hoc tests (Tukey tests) were carried out to see the between-group differences.

Table 7.10 shows that resource and ability are the only risk attributes affected by the location of the container terminal, as the *p*-value is smaller than 0.05. By looking at the post-hoc test in Table 7.11, terminals in China have a 1.93922 higher mean attribute score in resource and ability attribute. Also, terminals from other locations (apart from Hong Kong and China) are having a higher mean resource and ability concern than the terminals in Southeast Asia. Apart from resource and ability, the *p*-value in subjective norm attribute is 0.066, which is very close to the threshold of 0.05.

Table 7.12 shows that there are no significance differences among various concerns for different customer base, as no *t*-tests have *p*-value less than 0.05.

Table 7.13 reveals that with the difference in shareholding, the subjective norm concerns are likely to be different, with *p*-value smaller than 0.05. Table 7.14 shows that state-owned container terminals are more concerned about subjective norm than are privately owned container terminals (mean difference = 1.99259). Also, joint-venture container terminals are also more likely to pay more attention to subjective norm than are privately owned container terminals (mean difference = 2.26458).

Management composition differences are likely to impose more common practices on concerns about risk management. With *p*-value less than 0.05 as in Table 7.15, difference in management composition leads to a difference in attribute concerns over perceived cost, perceived efficacy, goal and objective, resource and ability and perceived image.

Table 7.10 ANOVA for location and risk attribute concerns

		Sum of Squares	df	Mean Square	F	Sig.
Probability	Between Groups	1.847	3	.616	.119	.948
	Within Groups	134.084	26	5.157		
	Total	135.931	29			
Severity	Between Groups	2.152	3	.717	.182	.908
	Within Groups	102.422	26	3.939		
	Total	104.574	29			
Cost	Between Groups	3.278	3	1.093	.497	.687
	Within Groups	57.130	26	2.197		
	Total	60.407	29			
Efficacy	Between Groups	4.962	3	1.654	.665	.581
	Within Groups	64.705	26	2.489		
	Total	69.667	29			
Goal and Objective	Between Groups	8.772	3	2.924	1.067	.380
	Within Groups	71.255	26	2.741		
	Total	80.027	29			
Resource and Ability	Between Groups	22.190	3	7.397	4.643	*.010*
	Within Groups	41.417	26	1.593		
	Total	63.607	29			
Perceived Image	Between Groups	7.840	3	2.613	1.431	.256
	Within Groups	47.490	26	1.827		
	Total	55.330	29			
Subjective Norm	Between Groups	17.018	3	5.673	2.700	.066
	Within Groups	54.631	26	2.101		
	Total	71.649	29			

Referring to Table 7.16, semi-international terminals have a higher perceived cost concern (mean differences = 2.0348, 1.83095) and a higher perceived image concern (mean differences = 1.29304, 2.02381) than do fully international or local container terminals. Furthermore, semi-international container terminals have higher concerns over the perceived efficacy, goal and objective, resource and ability (mean difference: 1.99286, 2.01667, 1.75952, respectively) than do local container terminals. Generally speaking, semi-international terminals have a higher concern than other terminals in all five aspects.

Table 7.17 shows that the terminal size also affects the concern over subjective norm. As shown in Table 7.18, large container terminals are likely to have greater concern over the subjective norm than are the small container terminals (mean difference = 2.07143).

Table 7.11 Post-hoc test for location and resources and ability attribute

Dependent Variable	(I) Location	(J) Location	Mean Difference (I-J)	Std. Error	Sig.
Resource and Ability	Hong Kong	China	−1.70588	.70139	.096
		S.E. Asia	.23333	.84666	.993
		Others	−1.87500	.89246	.179
	China	Hong Kong	1.70588	.70139	.096
		S.E. Asia	1.93922	.64210	*.027*
		Others	−.16912	.70139	.995
	S.E. Asia	Hong Kong	−.23333	.84666	.993
		China	−1.93922*	.64210	*.027*
		Others	−2.10833	.84666	.085
	Others	Hong Kong	1.87500	.89246	.179
		China	.16912	.70139	.995
		S.E. Asia	2.10833	.84666	.085

Table 7.12 Independent *t*-test for customer base and risk attribute concerns

	Equal Variances	F	Sig.	t	df	Sig. (2-tailed)	Mean Diff.	Std. Error Diff.
Probability	assumed	.665	.422	1.697	28	.101	1.53727	.90565
	not assumed			1.942	12.638	.075	1.53727	.79164
Severity	assumed	.306	.585	.025	28	.980	.02070	.83421
	not assumed			.029	13.564	.977	.02070	.70541
Cost	assumed	.188	.668	.877	28	.388	.54865	.62550
	not assumed			.955	11.473	.359	.54865	.57462
Efficacy	assumed	.380	.542	−.504	28	.618	−.34161	.67783
	not assumed			−.555	11.723	.589	−.34161	.61552
Goal and Objective	assumed	.317	.578	−.808	28	.426	−.58282	.72141
	not assumed			−.858	10.984	.409	−.58282	.67903
Resource and Ability	assumed	1.920	.177	−.022	28	.982	−.01449	.65061
	not assumed			−.027	13.867	.979	−.01449	.54473
Perceived Image	assumed	.013	.910	−1.974	28	.058	−1.12215	.56854
	not assumed			−2.143	11.421	.054	−1.12215	.52357
Subj. Norm	assumed	2.247	.145	−.272	28	.788	−.18737	.68961
	not assumed			−.416	25.887	.681	−.18737	.45046

Table 7.13 ANOVA for shareholding structure and risk attribute concerns

		Sum of Squares	df	Mean Square	F	Sig.
Probability	Between Groups	5.502	2	2.751	.569	.572
	Within Groups	130.429	27	4.831		
	Total	135.931	29			
Severity	Between Groups	1.003	2	.502	.131	.878
	Within Groups	103.571	27	3.836		
	Total	104.574	29			
Cost	Between Groups	.768	2	.384	.174	.841
	Within Groups	59.640	27	2.209		
	Total	60.407	29			
Efficacy	Between Groups	9.038	2	4.519	2.013	.153
	Within Groups	60.629	27	2.246		
	Total	69.667	29			
Goal and Objective	Between Groups	5.793	2	2.896	1.053	.363
	Within Groups	74.234	27	2.749		
	Total	80.027	29			
Resource and Ability	Between Groups	7.516	2	3.758	1.809	.183
	Within Groups	56.092	27	2.077		
	Total	63.607	29			
Perceived Image	Between Groups	9.512	2	4.756	2.803	.078
	Within Groups	45.818	27	1.697		
	Total	55.330	29			
Subjective Norm	Between Groups	19.986	2	9.993	5.223	*.012*
	Within Groups	51.663	27	1.913		
	Total	71.649	29			

Table 7.14 Post-hoc test for shareholding structure and subjective norm

Dependent Variable	(I)Location	(J)Location	Mean Difference (I-J)	Std. Error	Sig.
Subjective Norm	State-Owned	Joint Venture	−.27199	.57636	.885
		Private	1.99259*	.77155	*.040*
	Joint Venture	State-Owned	.27199	.57636	.885
		Private	2.26458*	.70871	*.010*
	Private	State-Owned	−1.99259*	.77155	*.040*
		Joint Venture	−2.26458*	.70871	*.010*

Table 7.15 ANOVA for management composition and risk attribute concerns

		Sum of Squares	df	Mean Square	F	Sig.
Probability	Between Groups	24.210	2	12.105	2.925	.071
	Within Groups	111.721	27	4.138		
	Total	135.931	29			
Severity	Between Groups	14.952	2	7.476	2.252	.125
	Within Groups	89.622	27	3.319		
	Total	104.574	29			
Cost	Between Groups	20.562	2	10.281	6.966	**.004**
	Within Groups	39.846	27	1.476		
	Total	60.407	29			
Efficacy	Between Groups	16.387	2	8.194	4.152	**.027**
	Within Groups	53.280	27	1.973		
	Total	69.667	29			
Goal and Objective	Between Groups	16.754	2	8.377	3.575	**.042**
	Within Groups	63.273	27	2.343		
	Total	80.027	29			
Resource and Ability	Between Groups	12.940	2	6.470	3.448	**.046**
	Within Groups	50.668	27	1.877		
	Total	63.607	29			
Perceived Image	Between Groups	16.943	2	8.471	5.958	**.007**
	Within Groups	38.387	27	1.422		
	Total	55.330	29			
Subjective Norm	Between Groups	2.298	2	1.149	.447	.644
	Within Groups	69.351	27	2.569		
	Total	71.649	29			

(c) Company characteristics and risk response

In order to analyse the differences among risk responses of various container terminal companies, correspondence analysis was carried out. It is an exploring task that aims to give ideas on the usage diversity of responses and the intensity of seeking external help. The company background information is used as the analysing variables.

On the other hand, two factors of interest (usage diversity of responses: 1–4) which represent the number of responses type being used from the choice of acceptance, reduce, reduce both and sharing; intensity to seek external help (overall usage of sharing responses among the 7 risk categories): 1: solely internal – no sharing being used, 2: minimal external help – one category relies on the use of sharing, 3: certain degree of external help – two categories rely on the use

Table 7.16 Post-hoc test for management composition and other risk attributes

Dependent Variable	(I)Location	(J)Location	Mean Difference (I-J)	Std. Error	Sig.
Cost	Full International	Semi-International	−2.03480*	.56951	*.004*
		Local	−.20385	.51098	.916
	Semi-International	Full International	2.03480*	.56951	*.004*
		Local	1.83095*	.59867	*.013*
	Local	Full International	.20385	.51098	.916
		Semi-International	−1.83095*	.59867	*.013*
Efficacy	Full International	Semi-International	−1.10440	.65856	.232
		Local	.88846	.59087	.305
	Semi-International	Full International	1.10440	.65856	.232
		Local	1.99286*	.69227	*.020*
	Local	Full International	−.88846	.59087	.305
		Semi-International	−1.99286*	.69227	*.020*
Goal and Objective	Full International	Semi-International	−1.15385	.71766	.260
		Local	.86282	.64390	.386
	Semi-International	Full International	1.15385	.71766	.260
		Local	2.01667*	.75440	*.033*
	Local	Full International	−.86282	.64390	.386
		Semi-International	−2.01667*	.75440	.033
Resource and Ability	Full International	Semi-International	−.87363	.64221	.375
		Local	.88590	.57620	.290
	Semi-International	Full International	.87363	.64221	.375
		Local	1.75952*	.67509	*.038*
	Local	Full International	−.88590	.57620	.290
		Semi-International	−1.75952*	.67509	*.038*
Perceived Image	Full International	Semi-International	−1.29304	.55899	*.071*
		Local	.73077	.50154	.327
	Semi-International	Full International	1.29304	.55899	*.071*
		Local	2.02381*	.58761	*.005*
	Local	Full International	−.73077	.50154	.327
		Semi-International	−2.02381*	.58761	*.005*

of sharing, 4: extensive external help – three or more categories rely on the use of sharing) are put into the joint plot of category points (Figure 7.6). The relative distances between the category points (company characteristics) and the object points (usage diversity and intensity for external help) can be compared to see the preferences and choices on responses of the companies under investigation.

Points close to the origin represent the common or most frequent observations towards particular categories or objects, and it indicates that the container

Table 7.17 ANOVA for terminal size and risk attribute concerns

		Sum of Squares	df	Mean Square	F	Sig.
Probability	Between Groups	4.274	2	2.137	.438	.650
	Within Groups	131.656	27	4.876		
	Total	135.931	29			
Severity	Between Groups	3.373	2	1.687	.450	.642
	Within Groups	101.201	27	3.748		
	Total	104.574	29			
Cost	Between Groups	9.373	2	4.687	2.479	.103
	Within Groups	51.034	27	1.890		
	Total	60.407	29			
Efficacy	Between Groups	5.709	2	2.854	1.205	.315
	Within Groups	63.958	27	2.369		
	Total	69.667	29			
Goal and Objective	Between Groups	.412	2	.206	.070	.933
	Within Groups	79.614	27	2.949		
	Total	80.027	29			
Resource and Ability	Between Groups	.757	2	.379	.163	.851
	Within Groups	62.850	27	2.328		
	Total	63.607	29			
Perceived Image	Between Groups	2.084	2	1.042	.528	.596
	Within Groups	53.246	27	1.972		
	Total	55.330	29			
Subjective Norm	Between Groups	19.601	2	9.801	5.084	*.013*
	Within Groups	52.048	27	1.928		
	Total	71.649	29			

terminal companies usually rely on internal efforts to solve risk-related problems (as shown by the solely internal object point near the origin and the farthest distance from the origin for extensive external help). These companies usually use two different types of risk responses to tackle the risk problems. One of them is likely to be sharing, or "share" in the definition of this book. This is because the two object points are nearly overlapping each other. "Certain degree of external help" means that the companies have made use of the sharing response in some risk categories. Full diversification of response usage which makes use of all types of risk responses is less favoured by most of the terminals. The object point "extensive external help" is farthest from the origin, and it shows that container terminal companies are very unlikely to share their risk with external parties on a large scale.

Table 7.18 Post-hoc test for terminal size and subjective norm

Dependent Variable	(I) Location	(J) Location	Mean Difference (I-J)	Std. Error	Sig.
Subjective Norm	> 70,000 DWT	10–70K DWT	.83333	.58400	.342
		< 10,000 DWT	2.07143*	.65090	*.010*
	10–70K DWT	> 70,000 DWT	–.83333	.58400	.342
		< 10,000 DWT	1.23810	.68422	.186
	< 10,000 DWT	> 70,000 DWT	–2.07143*	.65090	*.010*
		10–70K DWT	–1.23810	.68422	.186

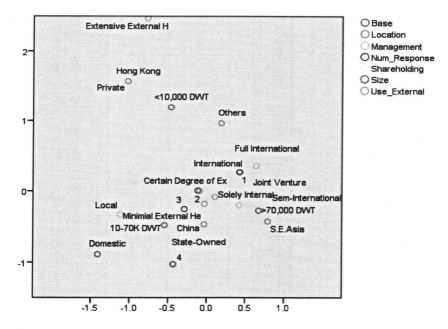

Figure 7.6 Joint plot of category points for risk response and company characteristic

Combining the results in Figures 7.6 and 7.7 provides a more detailed explanation of the difference in risk-response choices. Referring to the discrimination measures, the choices on the number of responses used are affected by management composition and customer base. Joint venture terminals with an international customer base are more likely to demonstrate a tendency of using a single response or minimal diversification responses. On the other hand, the

Discrimination Measures

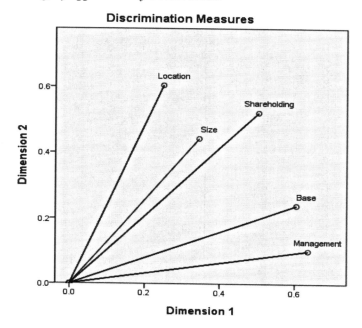

Figure 7.7 Discrimination measure (by graphical approach)

intensity of seeking external help is more likely caused by the difference in location. Hong Kong terminals are more likely to use more external help.

7.3 Findings relating to risk response, risk attribute and risk category

The previous section focuses on the overall direction of risk measures determination. Rationale for risk decisions is revealed at the companywide level. Here, the risk attribute considerations for determining response to a particular risk category are analysed. First, tests are carried out to show the influence of risk attributes on the risk-response choices. Then the risk attributes and the risk responses are analysed to see if the concerns are different for different risk categories.

(a) Risk response and risk attribute

In order to find out the impact of risk attributes on the choice of risk responses, a multinomial regression is carried out. The risk responses are divided into four different types (reduce both, reduce, accept and share), and thus there are four nominal levels (as shown in H2i). Accordingly, the eight attributes to be studied (i: 1: probability, 2: severity, 3: perceived cost, 4: perceived efficacy, 5: goal and objective, 6: resource and ability, 7: perceived image, 8: subjective norm) are extracted from the SURE model.

Table 7.19 Overall model significance for multinomial regression model

Model	Model Fitting Criteria	Likelihood Ratio Tests		
	−2 Log Likelihood	Chi-Square	df	Sig.
Intercept Only	335.070			
Final	290.270	44.801	24	.006

In order to make use of the model for the analysis, the overall model signifi-cance needs to be tested. Table 7.19 shows that the *p*-value is less than 0.05 (*p*-value = 0.006), which demonstrates that the model is significant for further interpretation. Then Table 7.20 is used for testing the relationship significance between the independent variables (attributes) and the dependent variable (response). Through this analysis, it is found that the two attributes goal and objective and subjective norm are significant at 0.05 level of significance, with *p*-value equal to 0.017 and 0.002, respectively.

Table 7.21 is constructed to further evaluate their influence on the risk responses. The "reduce both" option is used as the reference category. First, by looking at the "reduce" option relative to the "reduce both" group, goal and objective is significant, and the value of Exp(B) is 2.672. This implies that for each unit increase in goal and objective, the odds increase by (2.672−1 =1.672). In other words, for each unit increase in goal and objective, the odds of choosing "reduce" increase by 167.2%. Decision makers who pay more attention to goal and objective attribute are more likely to choose "reduce" rather than "reduce both" as a risk response.

Similar logic can be applied to the subjective norm attribute. Referring to Table 7.20, it is found that decision makers who pay less attention to subjective norm are more likely to choose responses other than "reduce both". Based on this theorem, it implies that the "reduce both" option involves decision makers who pay more attention to the subjective norm attribute. Specifically, with one unit increase in subjective norm, the odds of choosing "reduce", "accept" and "share" decrease by 37.1% (1 − 0.639 = 0.371), 30.3% (1 − 0.697 = 0.303) and 31.3% (1 − 0.687 = 0.313), respectively.

Although perceived image is not significant overall, it is found that decision makers displaying higher concern on perceived image are less likely to choose "share" in comparison to "reduce both". To conclude, only $H2_5$ and $H2_8$ are rejected in this analysis.

(b) Risk response and risk category

The possible relationships between the risk category and the risk response are shown by using the correspondence analysis. The risk categories include natural disaster, external event, accident caused by staff, equipment, it system and social

Table 7.20 Likelihood ratio tests for risk attributes and risk responses

Effect	Model Fitting Criteria	Likelihood Ratio Tests		
	−2 Log Likelihood of Reduced Model	Chi-Square	df	Sig.
Intercept	291.289	1.019	3	.797
Probability	294.430	4.161	3	.245
Severity	291.538	1.269	3	.737
Perceived Cost	296.521	6.252	3	.100
Perceived Efficacy	293.519	3.250	3	.355
Goal and Objective	300.497	10.228	3	.017
Resource and Ability	293.080	2.811	3	.422
Perceived Image	296.375	6.106	3	.107
Subjective Norm	304.600	14.331	3	.002

Table 7.21 Multinomial regression model for H2i

Response		B	Std. Error	Wald	df	Sig.	Exp(B)
Reduce	Intercept	−.471	1.679	.079	1	.779	
	Probability	.333	.312	1.140	1	.286	1.395
	Severity	−.350	.407	.740	1	.390	.705
	Perceived Cost	.650	.384	2.871	1	.090	1.916
	Perceived Efficacy	−.614	.371	2.732	1	.098	.541
	Goal and Objective	.983	.417	5.550	1	.018	2.672
	Resource and Ability	−.509	.324	2.466	1	.116	.601
	Perceived Image	−.465	.326	2.036	1	.154	.628
	Subjective Norm	−.448	.209	4.574	1	.032	.639
Accept	Intercept	.518	1.082	.229	1	.632	
	Probability	−.157	.121	1.689	1	.194	.855
	Severity	−.119	.193	.382	1	.537	.888
	Perceived Cost	.349	.203	2.947	1	.086	1.418
	Perceived Efficacy	−.142	.192	.548	1	.459	.867
	Goal and Objective	.385	.229	2.824	1	.093	1.469
	Resource and Ability	−.061	.206	.087	1	.768	.941
	Perceived Image	−.248	.212	1.368	1	.242	.780
	Subjective Norm	−.361	.136	7.008	1	.008	.697

Response		B	Std. Error	Wald	df	Sig.	Exp(B)
Share	Intercept	.846	1.017	.693	1	.405	
	Probability	−.093	.118	.623	1	.430	.911
	Severity	.042	.192	.048	1	.826	1.043
	Perceived Cost	.180	.176	1.047	1	.306	1.198
	Perceived Efficacy	.019	.193	.009	1	.924	1.019
	Goal and Objective	.378	.227	2.766	1	.096	1.459
	Resource and Ability	−.154	.194	.629	1	.428	.857
	Perceived Image	−.405	.198	4.189	1	.041	.667
	Subjective Norm	−.375	.131	8.178	1	*.004*	.687

Note: The reference category is "Reduce Both"

and human issues (as defined in previous chapters). The risk responses are the four options used in the previous sections (reduce both, reduce, accept and share).

Some patterns are identified from the correspondence analysis as shown in Figure 7.8. First, "reduce" is the most commonly used risk response when faced with external event, and their relationship is very standard in risk-response choices (both points are close to the origin). Second, when facing social and human risks, surprisingly, decision makers tend to choose to accept the consequences. Third, for accidents caused by staff, decision makers tend to tackle them by adopting the "reduce both" option. Other risk responses and risk categories do not demonstrate any particular pattern, as shown by the scatterpoints in the graph.

(c) Risk category and risk attribute

For investigating the possible relationships between risk attributes and risk categories, one ANOVA is carried out for each of the six categories. The eight risk attributes are used as the dependent variables, while the risk categories are used as group variables. The hypotheses are defined as H3i (i: 1: probability, 2: severity, 3: perceived cost, 4: perceived efficacy, 5: goal and objectives, 6: resource and ability, 7: perceived image, 8: subjective norm).

Table 7.22 shows that with 0.05 level of significance, $H3_6$ and $H3_7$ are rejected. There is a difference in the concerns for resource and ability and for perceived image over the risk categories.

However, when we take a closer look at the mean attribute differences with resource and ability as the dependent variable (Table 7.23), even for a group with overall significance, there is a little difference in the score (concerns). The level of significance has been set at 0.1 in order to see the difference in resource and ability. By then, the result indicates that decision makers are more likely to

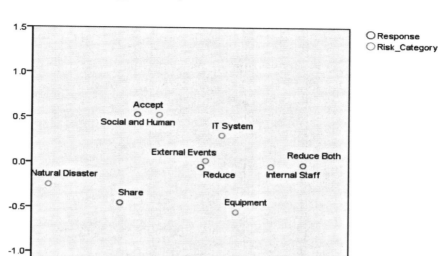

Figure 7.8 Correspondence analysis for response and risk category

have higher concern on resource and ability when facing accidents caused by Equipment failure than those caused by external event (mean difference = 1.233).

Similarly, by relaxing the level of significance to 0.1, there are three risk categories demonstrating differences in the mean scores (Table 7.24) when perceived image is adopted as the dependent variable. Here, decision makers tend to pay more attention to perceived image when facing accidents caused by staff or social and human issues, than those inferred by natural disaster (mean differences are 1.267 and 1.467 respectively).

7.4 Factors in effective risk management

The preceding two sections have demonstrated the risk practices of terminal operators. However, common practices do not imply the best practices. In this section, several performance measures are used to reveal the underlying attributes, rationale and responses that are highly related to effective risk management in container terminal operations. Variables that can lead to a substantial decrease in probability and severity of the risk are discovered. As the dependent variables for each of the models are binary, logistic regression is used in the analysis.

Table 7.22 ANOVA for risk category and risk attribute

		Sum of Squares	df	Mean Square	F	Sig.
Probability	Between Groups	57.183	5	11.437	1.760	.123
	Within Groups	1130.567	174	6.498		
	Total	1187.750	179			
Severity	Between Groups	13.178	5	2.636	.537	.748
	Within Groups	854.600	174	4.911		
	Total	867.778	179			
Cost	Between Groups	7.778	5	1.556	.464	.803
	Within Groups	583.667	174	3.354		
	Total	591.444	179			
Perceived Efficacy	Between Groups	16.933	5	3.387	.905	.479
	Within Groups	651.067	174	3.742		
	Total	668.000	179			
Goal and Objective	Between Groups	26.761	5	5.352	1.336	.251
	Within Groups	696.900	174	4.005		
	Total	723.661	179			
Resource and Ability	Between Groups	40.711	5	8.142	2.626	.026
	Within Groups	539.600	174	3.101		
	Total	580.311	179			
Perceived Image	Between Groups	53.178	5	10.636	3.174	.009
	Within Groups	583.133	174	3.351		
	Total	636.311	179			
Subjective Norm	Between Groups	21.894	5	4.379	1.241	.292
	Within Groups	614.167	174	3.530		
	Total	636.061	179			

(a) Probability reduction in risk category

In this section, the main focus is the effect of risk attributes (H4aj) and risk responses (H4b) on probability reduction. But effects of company background and uncontrollable factors on efficient handling of risk responses are also analysed (H4cj).

Risk attributes analysis includes the average score for the eight attributes; therefore, H4aj (j: 1: probability, 2: severity, 3: perceived cost, 4: perceived efficacy, 5: goal and objectives, 6: resource and ability, 7: perceived image, 8: subjective norm). Risk response analysis includes responses used to tackle the event H4b (use of reduce both or reduce). Company background involves five elements, H4cj (j: 1: location [of the terminal[, 2: customer base, 3: shareholding [structure], 4: management [composition], 5: terminal size, 6: risk category). For each

Table 7.23 Post-hoc test for risk category and resource and ability

Dependent Variable	(I) Risk Category	(J) RiskCategory	Mean Difference (I-J)	Std. Error	Sig.
Resource and Ability	Natural Disaster	External Events	.267	.455	.992
		Internal Staff	−.900	.455	.358
		Equipment	−.967	.455	.279
		IT System	−.867	.455	.402
		Social and Human	−.400	.455	.951
	External Event	Natural Disaster	−.267	.455	.992
		Internal Staff	−1.167	.455	.111
		Equipment	−1.233	.455	*.078*
		IT System	−1.133	.455	.132
		Social and Human	−.667	.455	.686
	Staff	Natural Disaster	.900	.455	.358
		External Events	1.167	.455	.111
		Equipment	−.067	.455	1.000
		IT System	.033	.455	1.000
		Social and Human	.500	.455	.881
	Equipment	Natural Disaster	.967	.455	.279
		External Events	1.233	.455	*.078*
		Internal Staff	.067	.455	1.000
		IT System	.100	.455	1.000
		Social and Human	.567	.455	.813
	IT System	Natural Disaster	.867	.455	.402
		External Events	1.133	.455	.132
		Internal Staff	−.033	.455	1.000
		Equipment	−.100	.455	1.000
		Social and Human	.467	.455	.909
	Social and Human	Natural Disaster	.400	.455	.951
		External Events	.667	.455	.686
		Internal Staff	−.500	.455	.881
		Equipment	−.567	.455	.813
		IT System	−.467	.455	.909

category of variables, the last category is used as the reference category. (That is, response: reduce; location: others; customer base: international; shareholding: private; management: local; terminal size: < 10,000 DWT; risk category: social and human). As the average decrease in probability is around 26%, if the company is able to decrease the probability by more than 30%, a value of 1 will be given to the dependent variable. For better interpretation, the level of significance is relaxed to 0.1.

Table 7.24 Post-hoc test for risk category and perceived image

Dependent Variable	(I) Risk Category	(J) Risk Category	Mean Difference (I-J)	Std. Error	Sig.
Perceived Image	Natural Disaster	External Events	−.500	−.500	.897
		Internal Staff	−1.267	−1.267	.085
		Equipment	−.233	−.233	.996
		IT System	−1.067	−1.067	.218
		Social and Human	−1.467	−1.467	.027
	External Events	Natural Disaster	.500	.500	.897
		Internal Staff	−.767	−.767	.585
		Equipment	.267	.267	.993
		IT System	−.567	−.567	.837
		Social and Human	−.967	−.967	.321
	Internal Staff	Natural Disaster	1.267	1.267	.085
		External Events	.767	.767	.585
		Equipment	1.033	1.033	.250
		IT System	.200	.200	.998
		Social and Human	−.200	−.200	.998
	Equipment	Natural Disaster	.233	.233	.996
		External Events	−.267	−.267	.993
		Internal Staff	−1.033	−1.033	.250
		IT System	−.833	−.833	.492
		Social and Human	−1.233	−1.233	.100
	IT System	Natural Disaster	1.067	1.067	.218
		External Events	.567	.567	.837
		Internal Staff	−.200	−.200	.998
		Equipment	.833	.833	.492
		Social and Human	−.400	−.400	.958
	Social and Human	Natural Disaster	1.467	1.467	.027
		External Events	.967	.967	.321
		Internal Staff	−.500	.200	.998
		Equipment	−.567	1.233	.100
		IT System	−.467	.400	.958

Referring to Table 7.25, Models 1, 2 and 3 are built to incorporate only a specific group of variables (Model 1 is for attributes, Model 2 is for response, Model 3 is for uncontrollable factor and company background). The low chi-square figures, which demonstrate the low fitness of the model, are treated as the base models for comparing and contrasting the results for the remaining models. Despite that, all three models are significant at 0.05 level of significance.

Model 4 combines the attribute with the response choice. From this, it is found that severity, perceived efficacy, resource and ability, subjective norm and risk response are significant. However, the fitness level is similar, and there is no significance reduction of –2LL.

Model 5 combines the response choice with the uncontrollable factors. Risk response is still significant, while the location, management composition and risk category demonstrate certain effects on the decrease in probability of occurrence for the risk event. Also, partial effect for the terminal size on the decrease in occurrence is worth noting, although the overall significance for the variable is not present.

Model 6 combines the risk attributes with the uncontrollable factors. It is found that severity, perceived efficacy and subjective norm are significant. Furthermore, it is also identified that only location (of the terminal) has an overall significance. Unlike Model 5, shareholding structure and management composition do not constitute an overall significance towards the risk occurrence reduction. This model is preferable, as the hit rate is the same as Model 5, and the chi-square value is not high, but the degree of freedom is significantly increased compared to Model 5.

Model 7 is a full model which combines all variables under consideration and reveals that severity, efficacy and subjective norm are the significant risk attributes. Risk response category is not significant. Location (of the terminal) and management composition have some effects on the reduction in risk occurrence. Response choice is also critical in the risk reduction. The results in this model are very similar to the previous models. Nevertheless, this model is useful for drawing the conclusion for hypothesis, as it includes all variables, and the fitness statistic is the highest (104.268), with the highest hit rate (87.8%) and highest reduction in –2LL.

The analysis indicates that the higher is the focus on severity, the less likely is the container terminal company to achieve a significant reduction in the occurrence of the risk event. Similar logic applies to subjective norm. If the container terminal company pays more attention to subjective norm, it is less likely to achieve a good reduction in occurrence of the risk event. However, if the container terminal company pays more attention to the perceived efficacy, it has a higher chance to reduce occurrence of the incident.

Hong Kong and Southeast Asia container terminal companies are less efficient in terms of probability reduction than other terminals in this study. Furthermore, full international and semi-international container terminal companies have lower probability-reduction records compared to fully local companies.

Though the size of the terminal does not contribute to an overall significant difference in risk handling, it is worth noting that medium-sized container terminals do perform better than small container terminals in probability reduction of risk events. Moreover, the risk category does not contribute to a reduction difference as expected.

(b) Severity reduction in risk category

Risk attributes analysis includes the average score for the eight attributes, therefore, H5aj (j: 1: probability, 2: severity, 3: perceived cost, 4: perceived efficacy, 5: goal and objective, 6: resource and ability, 7: perceived image, 8: subjective norm). Risk responses analysis includes responses used to tackle the event H5b (use of reduce both or share). Company background involves five elements, H5cj (j: 1: location [of the terminal], 2: customer base, 3: shareholding [structure], 4: management [composition], 5: terminal size, 6: risk category). The last category of variables is used as the reference category. (That is, response: sharing; location: others; customer base: international; shareholding: private; management: local; terminal size: < 10,000 DWT; risk category: social and human.) As the average decrease in severity is less than 30%, if the company is able to decrease the severity by more than 30%, a value of 1 is given to the dependent variable. For better interpretation, the level of significance is relaxed to 0.1.

Referring to Table 7.26, Model 2 is not significant (0.259), and therefore it is discarded. This may hint that the risk response choice is not significant in severity reduction. Again, Model 1 and Model 3 with single sets of variables are used as the base models for comparison.

Model 4 combines the attributes with the risk response choices, with severity and perceived efficacy the only variables that are significant in the model. The classification is rather low, and the model is only significant at 0.1 level of significance. The fitness of the model is also very low. Therefore, it is not a good choice of model.

Model 5 combines risk response choices with uncontrollable factors, and it reveals that only location (of the terminal) demonstrates an overall significance. The equipment risk category drags down the decrease in severity reduction compared to that of social and human risk category. That is to say, a lower severity reduction in the equipment risk category is likely to occur in comparison to that of the social and human risk category.

The only difference between Models 6 and 7 is the inclusion of risk response choice. Unlike the previous section on occurrence reduction, the risk response choice is not significant in either case. Model 7 shows only a slight improvement in model fit as shown by the chi-square figure. The reduction in –2LL is not substantial compared to that of Model 6. Also, the hit rate is lower than that of Model 6. It is always better to have a model with fewer predictors that still provides sufficient results. Therefore, conclusions for the hypotheses in this section are mainly drawn from the results derived from Model 6.

Model 6 shows that severity demonstrates a negative effect on the decrease in severity reduction. The higher the concern over severity, surprisingly, the lower the probability of having a significant reduction in severity. However, container terminal companies pay more attention to the perceived efficacy in order to achieve a higher reduction in severity. Furthermore, location (of the terminal)

Table 7.25 Alternative logistic regression models for probability reduction

	Model 1	Model 2	Model 3	Model 4	Model 5	Model 6	Model 7
Constant	.132	-1.946+	2.058	-2.286	-4.644+	1.597	-6.422
Probability	-.211			-.180		-.327	-.310
Severity	-.488*			-.573**		-.674*	-.600+
Cost	.192			.260		.229	.319
Efficacy	.825***			.822***		1.140***	1.075**
Goal	-.264			-.179		.076	-.050
Resources	.503**			.512**		.249	.490
Image	.080			.061		.211	.378
Norm	-.589**			-.712**		-.625+	-1.046**
Response (1)		2.358*		2.882*	9.045***		10.429**
Location			**		***	*	*
Location (1)			-2.317+		-4.849**	-1.492	-4.951*
Location (2)			-.417		-2.877*	1.078	-2.383
Location (3)			-3.427**		-7.308***	-3.276*	-8.900**
Base (1)			.910		-.500	-.335	-1.755
Shareholding							
Shareholding (1)			-1.372		-.326	-1.914	-.511
Shareholding (2)			-.520		1.337	-2.572+	.825

	(1)	(2)	(3)	(4)	(5)	(6)	(7)
Management				*			+
Management (1)			-.553		-3.142**	-1.680+	-5.753**
Management (2)			-.805		-3.033**	-1.563	-5.369*
Size							
Size (1)			.614		1.542+	.389	2.260
Size (2)			-.079		1.997*	.420	3.367+
Risk Category			+		*		
Risk Category (1)			-.167		-.688	-.779	-1.023
Risk Category (2)			.850		1.706+	.629	.926
Risk Category (3)			-.839		-1.174	-1.252	-1.582
Risk Category (4)			-.695		-.862	-.491	-.360
Risk Category (5)			1.004		1.391	.620	1.509
Chi square	7.413	39.279	45.918	47.281	76.680	80.329	104.268
-2LL	171.426	139.560	132.921	131.558	102.160	98.510	74.571
Hit rate	61.8	76.3	77.1	79.4	82.4	82.4	87.8
Model significance	0.006	.000	.000	.000	.000	.000	.000
Degree of freedom	1	8	15	9	16	23	24

+$p < .10$, *$p < .05$ **$p < .01$ ***$p < .001$

Table 7.26 Alternative logistic regression models for severity reduction

	Model 1	Model 2	Model 3	Model 4	Model 5	Model 6	Model 7
Constant	.004	−.310	2.132+	−.249	1.495	1.216	.763
Probability	.001			−.008		.203	.196
Severity	−.349*			−.349*		−.450+	−.475+
Cost	.016			.035		.199	.220
Efficacy	.317+			.315+		.669*	.673*
Goal	−.243			−.221		−.364	−.298
Resources	.316*			.311		−.083	−.087
Image	.111			.087		.175	.146
Norm	−.140			−.171		−.137	−.184
Response (1)		.489		.536	.759		.670
Location			*		*	*	*
Location (1)			−1.996+		−2.023	−1.779	−1.720
Location (2)			−1.072		−1.037	−.696	−.482
Location (3)			−3.792**		−3.728*	−3.749*	−3.484*
Base (1)			.782		1.041	.434	.615
Shareholding							
Shareholding (1)			.887		.764	1.340	1.137

Shareholding (2)			.148		-.118	-.229	-.543
Management						+	+
Management (1)			.592		.938	1.000	1.223
Management (2)			-.237		.150	-.869	-.645
Size							
Size (1)			-.420*		-.614	-.775	-.842
Size (2)			-.933		-1.085	-1.383	-1.515
Risk Category							
Risk Category (1)			-1.491		-1.253	-2.055*	-1.853*
Risk Category (2)			-.524		-.550	-.778	-.834
Risk Category (3)			-.897		-1.026	-.952	-1.082
Risk Category (4)			-1.160		-1.195+	-1.274	-1.360
Risk Category (5)			-.781		-.824	-1.108	-1.196
Chi square	15.335	1.274	50.206	16.539	51.547	68.108	68.927
-2LL	190.894	204.955	156.022	189.690	154.682	138.121	132.302
Hit rate	65.8	55.0	73.2	61.1	72.5	80.5	77.9
Model significance	.053	.259	.000	.056	.000	0.000	.000
Degree of freedom	8	1	15	9	16	23	24

$+p < .10, *p < .05 **p < .01 ***p < .001$

affects the reduction in severity, and container terminals in Southeast Asia are less likely to have a substantial reduction in severity compared to other terminals, excluding Hong Kong and Mainland China.

Management composition also imposes some effects to the decrease in severity, but the extent cannot be ascertained. Special attention is paid to natural disaster and social and human events, where the analysis shows that the reduction in severity for the former is harder than that of the latter risk category.

8 Risk management strategies in container terminals from the insight of the SURE model application

8.1 General observations and phenomena over existing risk-management practices in container terminals

Prior to the design of the questionnaire, the six categories of risk – namely, natural disaster, Accident caused by External Event, Accident caused by Staff, Breakdown/failure of Equipment, Breakdown/failure of IT system and Social and Human issues – were determined based on the experience of the author and verbal consultation with senior managements in the industry. Question 1 of the questionnaire was designed for proving the validity of these six categories of risk. Referring to Table 7.5, the six categories of risk are re-confirmed based on the replies of the respondents.

The implication of this finding is encouraging, mainly because many practitioners in the container terminal industry may not be able to categorize properly the operational risks they are facing: either they may not have sufficient experience to identify the risks, or there are too many risks involved in operational management that the practitioners are not able to classify systematically.

The replies to Question 2 of the questionnaire provide a good overview of the standard procedures that container terminal companies follow. With the limited time available for the respondents to provide their answers, the respondents may not have been able to list all related documentation. On the other hand, the responses to this question also provide another perspective for substantiating the validity of the six categories of operational risk defined in this study (see Table 7.6). Nevertheless, the author believes that most of the container terminal companies have a relatively complete set of standard procedures for dealing with various kinds of risks. The underlying reasons could be two-fold.

First, unlike the small and medium enterprises (SME), the capital investment of a container terminal is usually very high, as has been discussed earlier. With the huge amount of capital investment in place, the cost of employing competent people for managing risks is relatively low. To start with the basics of risk management, these competent people prepare series of guidelines and procedures so as to broadly educate the staff. Moreover, these guidelines and procedures also serve the purpose of relieving or reducing the liabilities of the company in case of accidents.

Second, all container terminal companies that the author has encountered are under the jurisdiction of their respective governments, mainly through the port authority, the port administration commission or a similar organization. The government officials working in these government organizations have a duty to maintain the safety standard of the port under their jurisdiction. In order not to bear the political liability and/or burden resulting from any accidents within the port, these officials carry out regular inspections of the container terminal companies. Apart from the on-site visits, documentation becomes another major area to be reviewed and checked by these officials. As such, almost all container terminal companies well prepare the documentation required to deal with these inspections.

Based on the responses to Question 3, most (more than 70%) of the container terminal companies can make decisions on risk management within days. This indicates that the container terminal industry in general does pay sufficient attention to risk management, especially for the operational risk that this study is focusing on.

Question 4 revealed the parties involved in selecting the treatment method for operational risk. Apart from the Operations Department that shall obviously be the main decision maker, almost all departments and people are involved in the decision-making process as per the results of this survey. That means that the management of operational risk is not limited to the people directly related to the physical operations of a container terminal but is in fact a companywide issue which all stakeholders in the company take part in.

Question 5 of the survey revealed the limitations affecting the management of a container terminal company in using the most "suitable" risk treatment method. According to the responses to the questionnaire, all eight attributes of the SURE model (namely probability, severity, perceived cost, perceived efficacy, goal and objective, resource and ability, perceived image and subjective norm) have been mentioned in the replies to various extents. Furthermore, as discussed in Section 7.01(b), although the word "probability" has not been explicitly mentioned by any of the respondents, the replies do indicate the respondents' understanding towards the importance of this attribute. This can be proved by some of the replies such as "inability to control the risk event", in that "inability" here implies the uncertainty of the probability of occurrence.

Other than the eight attributes of the SURE model, replies from respondents included many other issues and factors, but the reasons for not incorporating them into the SURE model have been discussed (see Table 7.4). Apart from those rare responses, the factor "laws, rules and regulations of the local government" has been mentioned by various respondents in different forms. If this factor has been so commonly considered by the respondents, this study shall have taken this into account when developing the SURE model.

However, according to the COSO ERM Framework, this factor "laws, rules and regulations of the local government" shall be classified in a much broader category of risk, which is the "Compliance Risk". If this factor is taken into consideration in the study of operational risk, then the demarcation between risk categories will become blurred, and it will easily be mixed up in the study with other unrelated or duplicated factors and/or attributes.

Question 6 asked about the measurement of the effectiveness of the risk treatment method. As expected by the author, this is one of the weakest areas in operational risk management of the container terminal companies. Apart from the risk categories that are directly related to equipment breakdown and IT system breakdown, the responses received from the respondents such as training frequency, regular emergency drills, measures borrowed from other operators and the like cannot in physical terms measure accurately the effectiveness of the risk treatment method. According to Figure 5.3, the measurement of the effectiveness of the risk treatment method shall be the change in coordinate (p and s) of the risk item with respect to the efforts and resources that the respondents have put in. The efforts and resources here could be in the form of money, people, time and so forth. This reinforces the author's belief that there is still plenty of room for improvement in the risk management knowledge of the stakeholders in the container terminal industry.

Referring to the replies to Question 7, most (87%) of the respondents have communicated with external parties before making decisions on risk response. These external parties include insurance companies, government authorities, legal advisors, consultants or even customers and other port companies. See also Table 7.9.

The replies to this question are not unpredictable. In fact, these replies can be further analysed according to the following. Insurers, legal advisors and consultants provide the concerned container terminal the common practice adopted in the industry, and the industry in fact includes mainly other terminals competing with them. Therefore these external parties could be grouped under the "Competitor" element. For when the government authorizes a given step, it will most of the time determine the policy and regulation, and it is similar to the goal and objective to be achieved but in a more macro sense. Furthermore, a certain portion of the terminals are partly owned by the government in various forms. Therefore, government authorities could also be regarded as "Shareholders" to a certain extent. As Customer has been mentioned by some respondents in answering this question, the three elements in the SURE model (Shareholder, Competitor and Customer) are covered here. With the "Organization" element being the internal entity and not external parties, responses to this question provide good support for the inclusion of the four elements in the SURE model.

When the respondents were asked about their knowledge of risk management as per Question 8 in the questionnaire, all of them replied that they possess knowledge of industry practice, and they also realize that their knowledge is limited and cannot cover all risk categories. The implication of this finding is that the practitioners of the container terminal industry do realize the complexity of the risks their business is facing. As such, more training and education in risk management shall be implemented throughout the industry.

Question 9 asked the respondents if the goals and objectives of the company affect their decisions on risk treatment methods. More than half of the respondents replied that the goals and objectives do affect their risk response decisions to some extent, and the impacts do vary among different risk categories. The remaining respondents replied that their risk-response decisions are already in line with the goals and objectives of the company. This gives very strong support to the argument that goal and objective is a very important attribute in risk evaluation, and therefore it obviously is one of the attributes in the SURE model so developed.

Question 10 of the survey asked whether the respondents would consider the impact to their company image when they made risk-response decisions. The results showed that 45% of the respondents would fully consider this factor when making the decision, while only 16% of the respondents replied that they would not consider this factor. The remaining 39% advised that they would consider the impact to company image to a certain extent.

That is to say, about 84% of the respondents would take the impact on company image into consideration when making risk-response decisions, either to a certain extent or to the fullest extent. This result is encouraging, as it proves that apart from the attributes mentioned before, company image is undoubtedly another important attribute for forming this newly developed SURE model.

Based on the replies to these 10 questions and the subsequent analysis, the SURE model as developed by the author is strongly supported. This provides a good foundation for the subsequent discussions.

8.2 Risk attribute and company characteristics

As per the discussion, the eight attributes (probability, severity, perceived cost, perceived efficacy, goal and objective, resource and ability, perceived image and subjective norm) in the SURE model are all proved to be valid. However, these attributes are affected by other factors to various extents. Based on the replies to the survey questionnaire, analysis of these relationships had been carried out. Some of the preliminary findings have been discussed in the previous chapters, and the following paragraphs discuss the possible underlying causes of these findings.

(a) Location

"Resource and ability" is a location-specific attribute in the SURE model, and this can be proved according to the results shown in Table 7.10. In the analysis, the respondents are separated into three different categories, which are Hong Kong, Mainland China and Southeast Asia. There are respondents from "other locations" as well. But since the sample size of these respondents is small, they are not taken into account in the further analysis.

The results of the analysis revealed that respondents from Mainland China have the highest concern for resource and ability when making the risk-response decision, while the difference between respondents from Hong Kong and Southeast Asia is not significant. The possible reasons for this phenomenon could be the tight budget in most of the container terminals in the Mainland and the "pass the buck" culture (pass the blame to someone else) that can easily be found in the Chinese community.

Even though the throughput volumes are high for container ports in the Mainland, not many of them can make a reasonable amount of profit that can justify their initial investment. This could be due to the fact that the ports in the Mainland are developed not purely based on the economic benefit of the investors but the macroeconomic gains of the community as a whole. Therefore, the main purpose of having a port in that particular location is not for making profit. As a result, the cash flow of the container terminals in the Mainland is usually tight. On the other hand, the management of these container terminal companies might blame inadequacy of resources for the consequences of any incident and failure to manage the operational risk. Therefore, they take resources and abilities seriously when making the risk-response decision.

(b) Customer base

This survey broadly separates the customers of container terminal companies into two major types, namely domestic and international. International customers means more than half of the containers the terminal handles are either imports from or exports to foreign countries. Otherwise they will be classified as domestic customers.

According to the analysis of the survey responses, the difference in customer base does not contribute to any significant impact to the risk-response decision made by the respondents. One possible reason for this phenomenon is that no matter what kinds of customers the respondents are facing, these customers demand almost the same post-incident treatment should there be any accident, and it will be difficult and not practical for the container terminal to discriminate among different kinds of customers.

(c) Shareholding structure

According to the result of this survey study, shareholding structure does play a role in affecting how the respondents consider subjective norm when they make the risk-response decision. For shareholding structure, three main categories are defined in this study, namely, state-owned, pure private investment or joint venture. In Hong Kong, the government only sets out the policies for port operations, and all container terminal companies in Hong Kong are owned by private investors. Container terminals in other locations are mainly joint-venture companies between local company(s) or government and the foreign investors. The reasons for joint venture companies being the majority (more than half) in this survey have been discussed in previous sections.

Shareholding structure affects how the respondents consider subjective norm, and the result indicates that the respondents from joint-venture and state-owned companies consider subjective norm to more or less the same extent when making risk-response decisions. On the other hand, respondents from privately owned companies pay less attention to subjective norm. One possible reason for this phenomenon is the pressure from shareholders, in particular the government-related shareholders. The ultimate objective of these government-related shareholders is not making profit, and they do worry that the container terminal company under their management is worse than similar background companies in the industry. As a result, they ensure the performance of their container terminal company, including the management, is not far behind the industry norm.

(d) Management composition

In this survey, management composition is broadly classified into three main categories: full international, which means three or more senior managers are expatriates, semi-international, which means one to two senior managers are expatriates, and local, which means no senior manager is expatriate.

Based on the results of answers of the respondents, it is revealed that the Management composition does affect the respondents' risk-response decision over five attributes, including perceived cost, perceived efficacy, goal and objective, resource and ability and perceived image. This is one of the major findings of this study, as this factor alone affects more than half of the attributes in the SURE model.

To get into details of the analysis of management composition, it is found that the respondents working in semi-international container terminal companies have a higher concern for perceived cost and perceived image than the other two types of management compositions.

Furthermore, it is also revealed that the respondents working in semi-international container terminal companies have a higher concern on perceived efficacy, goal and objective and resources and ability than do those in local terminals. But the differences between concerns of respondents working in semi-international companies and in full international companies are not significant.

The reason for this result is not a straightforward explanation due to the difference in management composition. Instead, we look at the circumstances that lead to the formation of a semi-international management.

It is a general belief that the employment of an expatriate, even though the remuneration package will usually be much higher than that of local employees, will bring better management and overall performance. In a semi-international company, the shareholder(s) on one hand believe and agree that management by expatriates will give better results. On the other hand, shareholders do not want to spend too much money in having many expatriates working in the organization. Cost and benefit are certainly the major considerations. Or else, there shall be more expatriates in the organization than just one or two.

With this background and working culture in place, people working in the organization unavoidably pay more attention to Cost, Efficacy and Resource when making decisions. Furthermore, a container terminal company with semi-international management composition will most likely be a joint-venture company that has more than one shareholder. In that case, the management of this kind of company will have to deal with and satisfy the requirements of more than one "boss". To avoid being blamed by any of the shareholders for unfair treatment or the like, the best strategy for the management is to have a clear goal and objective to follow.

Perceived image is another attribute that the respondents from semi-international container terminal companies pay higher attention to when making risk-response decisions. Perceived image mainly comes from how the customer sees the company in handling risk. The reason for this phenomenon is not obvious. However, based on the observations from the author, the reason for this phenomenon can be explained indirectly. First, fully international container terminal companies usually have already built up good relationships with customers through their parent company abroad, and therefore they need not worry too much about how the customer sees them as long as the management follows the guidelines and strategies of the parent company. Second, local container terminal companies might not consider the views of the customer their top priority mainly because they are backed by the local government to a certain extent. As such, the views of their backing entity, the local authority, might carry more weight when the management makes decisions. As a result, semi-international container terminal companies comparatively pay more attention to perceived image when making risk response decisions.

(e) Terminal size

Terminal size also affects one of the attributes in the SURE model. According to the analysis of survey results, it is noticed that subjective norm is affected by the size of the terminal when the respondents make risk-response decisions. In the questionnaire, we have classified the size of the container terminals into three categories based on the capability of the quay structure for berthing of container vessels, which are:

(a) capable of berthing 70,000 DWT or more vessels;
(b) capable of berthing 10,000 to 70,000 DWT vessels; and
(c) capable of berthing 10,000 DWT or fewer vessels.

The size of the vessels that a container terminal can accommodate reflects the scale of the terminal's quay structure, land area provided for container stacking and, in turn, their total capital investment and the size of the organization. That is to say, the larger the vessel that a container terminal can accommodate, the higher is the investment cost and the more the staff employed, and so is the office-based staff. Since there are more office-based staff in the organization, the container terminal company has more resources for obtaining information on external companies and competitors. Comparatively, it is difficult for a small container terminal company to know what other people are doing, at least not as easily as the large container terminal company does. As such, this concurs with the results of the questionnaire survey that the larger the terminal, the greater the concern about subjective norm when making the risk-response decisions.

8.3 Risk response and company characteristics

As discussed in Chapter 5 concerning how a risk item can be managed, the action that can be taken eventually falls into two forms – reduction in probability of occurrence and reduction in adverse consequence – even though the two forms can exist coincidently for the same risk item (i.e., Reduce Both). These two forms of action can be implemented either within the organization or with the help of external parties. For reducing the chance of occurrence, the external parties could be the entities such as the risk assessment consultant, safety consultant, safety auditor and risk management trainer. For reducing the adverse consequences of a risk event, the external parties could be the insurance company or broker.

If a container terminal company desires to make use of external entities for better managing risk, availability of suitable competent third parties is crucial. However, some of the respondents of this questionnaire survey are not located in well-developed cities, and therefore there may not be suitable competent third parties available for help locally.

On the other hand, engagement of external parties to provide assistance is not free, and the container terminal company shall be responsible for the extra cost so incurred, even though in the long run this extra cost could bring more benefits (or incur less expense in terms of loss) to the company as a whole. As a result, these container terminal companies prefer not to involve external entities. The analysis as shown in Section 7.02(c) does provide solid support to this argument.

Compared to other cities in Asia, Hong Kong is a well-developed, commercialized city (Japan is not included in this questionnaire survey and therefore is not analysed here). It is much easier for Hong Kong container terminal companies to seek various kinds of external assistance in risk management. Furthermore, container terminal companies in Hong Kong are comparatively more profitable, so they tend to engage more external assistance than others.

8.4 Relationship between risk attribute and risk response

(a) Goal and objective

It is revealed in Section 7.03(a) that the respondents who pay more attention to goal and objective would more likely choose "Reduce" rather than "Reduce Both". The difference between these two types of response is the action for reducing the severity of the adverse consequences resulting from the risk events.

Respondents who pay more attention to goal and objective fully understand that the sharing of risk does not reduce the chance of occurrence. If the goals and objectives of the company are to manage the risk, the best option is to reduce the chance of the risk events. Furthermore, transferring part of the risk consequence to others does come with a price to be borne by the organization eventually, one way or the other. This explains why the respondents who pay more attention to goal and objective will more likely select "Reduce" over "Reduce Both".

(b) Subjective norm

Despite the extra costs sharing of risk entails, risk responses "Share" and "Reduce Both" are the viable options to deal with different kinds of risks in real-life situations, especially where the chance of occurrence cannot be reduced pragmatically.

According to the findings in Section 7.03(a), respondents who pay more attention to subjective norm are more likely to choose the "Reduce Both" risk response. This finding is important in the sense that the more risk management information a container terminal company obtains from others, the higher the chance the management will select the "Reduce Both" risk response. The acquisition of risk management information from other container terminal companies will never be a one-way communication. While a container terminal company acquires risk management information from others, the counterpart will expect the same from them in return. By the same token, the more information is shared among container terminals, the more container terminals will choose "Reduce Both" risk response in the long run. **This implies that if the container terminal companies share more risk management information with others, there will be an overall reduction in risk exposure to the industry as a whole**.

(c) Perceived image

For perceived image, the analysis in Section 7.03(a) revealed that the higher the concern on perceived image, the higher the tendency of the respondents to choose the "Reduce Both" risk-response option more than the "Share" option.

As discussed earlier in this chapter, implementation of the "Share" option is comparatively easy as long as the company has the necessary resources, particularly the monetary resources (such as insurance premiums). However, the sharing of risk with other parties does not necessarily reflect the competence or the risk management capability of the container terminal companies, as it will not reduce the chance of risk occurrence. As a result, respondents who pay high attention to perceived image tend to choose the "Reduce Both" risk-response option so as to demonstrate to the customer their capability in reducing the chance of risk occurrence.

8.5 Relationship between risk category and risk response

(a) External event

Most of the respondents replied that they would choose "Reduce" as their risk response when dealing with an External Event. This is quite out of the expectation of the author. One possible reason for this phenomenon could be the respondents' belief in their ability to manage and control these artificial events. However, in reality, this kind of risk is also quite difficult to control, and the chance of occurrence is hard to reduce. Further study on this particular phenomenon is recommended.

(b) Social and human issues

As per the definition in this study, Social and Human issues refer to risks related to a larger community beyond the container terminal company itself, such as social unrest, labour strikes and the like. The root cause of this risk category mainly comes from the difference between the expected and the actual rewards of the people, particularly employees directly and indirectly employed by the company. In this study, it is revealed that most of the respondents choose to "Accept" this risk, meaning do nothing.

The reason for the management of container terminal companies to choose this take-no-action strategy is mainly because they might find it difficult to keep satisfying the needs of the employees, especially when labour unions are involved. The more the company gives up in a negotiation, the more the employees will ask for during the next negotiation, until one day the company can no longer sustain the business. Furthermore, even if precautionary measures have been taken by the employer or the management (such as the improvement of working conditions), these might not be taken into account during the subsequent negotiation, and eventually these measures become the "Hygiene Factors" as defined by Herzberg (1966).

(c) Accident caused by staff

For the risk category that includes Accidents caused by Staff, such as carelessness and misconduct, companies tend to believe they have the capability to reduce both the chance of occurrence and the severity when the accidents occur, that is, the "Reduce Both" risk response as per the definition in this study.

By delivering more promotion and education to staff, establishing proper procedures and policies or even implementing incentive schemes, the management considers it is possible to reduce the probability of the risk. Moreover, with the statutory requirement for enforcing various insurance policies relating to container terminal operations, such as employee compensation insurance and third-party liability insurance, the management assumes these insurance policies protect the company from any unexpected liabilities. That also means that the adverse consequence of the incident that falls into this category has been shared with external parties with the action of both reducing the chance of occurrence and the adverse consequence, and this is in line with the result of the questionnaire survey that this study has revealed.

8.6 Relationship between risk category and risk attribute

The analysis as shown in Section 7.03(c) reveals a few interesting phenomena in the relationship between risk categories and risk attributes. Since the analysis reveals no significant differences in most of the risk attributes except "resource and ability" and "perceived image", only these two attributes are discussed in the following paragraphs.

(a) *Resource and ability*

Respondents tend to pay more attention to resource and ability when dealing with Equipment Failure risk than with External Event risk. This can be explained by the fact that external events are comparatively hard to predict, and therefore there are not many precautionary measures the management can take in advance to prevent them from happening. On the other hand, by doing better preventive maintenance and regular checks, the management believes that the equipment shall perform better in terms of higher availability and shorter downtime. All these precautionary measures require resources (such as labour and cost) and ability (such as the technical competency of the equipment maintenance staff). It is therefore not difficult to understand the rationale for such a difference in respondents' preferences.

(b) *Perceived image*

Respondents tend to pay more attention to perceived image when dealing with Accident caused by Staff and Social and Human risk categories than when dealing with the natural disaster risk category.

Both Accident caused by Staff and Social and Human risk categories are related to the people that have direct relationships with the container terminal company, whilst the natural disaster risks are in general beyond the control of mankind. When dealing with natural disasters, companies can blame Mother Nature for the unexpected incidents, and there would be no reflection from her in return.

However, in the case of incidents related to people, the management's actions might induce consequential effects to the next moves of the counterparty. For example, a system of penalizing the staff member who has induced an incident may cause the staffer himself, or even the labour union, to undertake some extreme actions. If the situation goes sour, the management might be blamed for the actions that they have taken. As a result, the management will tend to pay more attention to perceived image when dealing with people issues, that is the Accident caused by Staff and Social and Human risk categories.

8.7 Effective risk management

As mentioned in the previous chapter, common practice does not mean the best practice. Here I would like to discuss some of the good practices that have been revealed from this study.

(a) *Reduction in probability*

There are a few findings which are related to low or lower probability of risk. First, the greater is the focus on severity, the less likely the company is able to achieve a significant reduction in risk occurrence, or probability. This relationship is comparatively obvious, as it relates to the cause and effect of the actions the company has taken.

Second, more attention to subjective norm usually cannot result in a substantial reduction in risk occurrence, that is, the probability for the risk to happen will not be reduced significantly. As mentioned in Section 7.03(a), companies paying more attention to subjective norm tend to choose a "Reduce Both" risk response instead of "Reduce". That also means that the management may not put all or most of the resources into reducing the chance of risk occurrence. As such, the reduction of risk occurrence will not be substantial.

Third, companies paying more attention to perceived efficacy usually have a higher chance to reduce the chance of occurrence. To analyse the efficacy of a risk response, the management has to study in detail various factors relating to the anticipated consequences, such as compensation to external parties, interruption to the business and so on. The study could involve plenty of data, statistics, tests and even pilot runs, and it also requires inputs from professionals and competent staff. Through these detailed studies, it will be easier for the management to identify the root causes of some of the risks, and thus it will help the management in identifying the proper means of reducing the occurrence of the risks.

Fourth, risk probability reduction for companies in well-developed cities like Hong Kong and other Southeast Asian countries has already taken place, and therefore the chance of further reduction in risk probability may not be as efficient or substantial. This phenomenon happens the same in the full international and semi-international companies, and the pure local companies have a higher chance to substantially reduce the risk probability, mainly because of their starting point of risk probability reduction.

Fifth, middle-sized container terminals (with berthing capacity from 10,000 to 70,000 DWT) do perform better than small container terminals in risk probability reduction. Larger container terminals usually have larger management teams, and so there will be more office-based staff. There will be more resources for handling operational risks, and thus the chance of reducing the probability of operational risk will be higher.

(b) Reduction in severity

Similar to those in probability, the findings relating to the lowering of severity are discussed next. First, the study shows that the higher the concern on the attribute "severity" (the severity before risk treatment is applied), the lower the chance of having a significant reduction in severity. Superficially, this is not in line with the general thought that the reduction of a particular risk shall be in direct proportion to how serious the management is. However, this is not as simple a case. The "significant reduction" in severity only measures the difference between the risk severity before and after the risk treatment is applied. In that case, if the severity has already been reduced through management strategy or other means, and the severity level is already low before the risk treatment method is applied, it is not uncommon to see that there will not be any "significant reduction" in severity.

Table 8.1 Overall summary of findings in this study

Subject	Findings	Reference
Eight Attributes in SURE model	The eight attributes are reinforced through the questionnaire survey	Table 7.3, Table 7.4 and Question 5 of Questionnaire
Six Categories of Risk in Terminal Operations	The six categories as defined in this research are confirmed appropriate	Table 7.5 and Qn. 1 of Questionnaire
Relationship between Company Characteristics and Risk Attribute	• Only resource and ability is significant	Table 7.10
	• Mainland China terminals have the highest concern on resource and ability	Table 7.11
	• No difference in risk attribute for customer base	Table 7.12
	• Subjective norm is affected by shareholding structure	Table 7.13
	• Joint Venture has the highest concern	Table 7.14
	• Perceived cost, perceived efficacy, goal and objective, resource and ability and perceived image affected by management composition	Table 7.15
	• Semi-international terminals have a higher overall concern	Table 7.16
	• Subjective norm is affected by Terminal Size	Table 7.17
	• Large terminal put more focus on subjective norm	Table 7.18
Seek External Assistance	Tend to use internal efforts to solve the risk related problems	Figure 7.6
Using more than one or more type of Risk Response	Number of different risk responses used is affected by management composition and customer base	Figure 7.7
Relationship between Risk Attribute and Risk Response	• Goal and Objective and subjective norm are significant	Table 7.20
	• Focus on Goal and Objective will tend to choose "Reduce"	Table 7.21
	• Focus on subjective norm will tend to choose "Reduce Both"	
	• Focus on perceived image, though not significant here, will less likely choose "Share" comparing to "Reduce Both"	

(*Continued*)

Table 8.1 (Continued)

Subject	Findings	Reference
Relationship between Risk Category and Risk Response	• Tend to choose "Reduce" for External Event • Tend to choose "Accept" for Social and Human issue • Tend to choose "Reduce Both" for accidents caused by Staff	Figure 7.8
Relationship between Risk Category and Risk Attribute	• Resource and Ability and perceived image are significant	Table 7.22
	• Higher concern in Resource and Ability for risks related Equipment and External Events	Table 7.23
	• Higher concern in perceived image for accident caused by Staff and Social and Human issue, than Natural Disaster	Table 7.24
Reduction in probability	• Higher focus on severity, less likely to reduce occurrence • Higher focus on subjective norm, less likely to reduce occurrence • Higher focus on perceived efficacy, higher chance to reduce occurrence • Terminals in Hong Kong and SE Asia are less efficient in reducing chance of occurrence • Local terminals have a higher chance to reduce chance of occurrence than full or semi international • Small terminal perform the worst in reducing chance of occurrence	Table 7.25
Reduction in severity	• Higher concern in severity, the lower the chance to reduce severity • Focus on perceived efficacy will have a higher chance to reduce severity • Terminals in SE Asia are less likely to reduce severity comparing to those in HK and China • Severity on social and human issue is more likely to be reduced comparing to natural disaster	Table 7.26
Overall Risk Reduction in the Industry	If individual terminals share and make known to others more risk management information, there will be an overall reduction in risk exposure as a whole	Section 8.04(b)

Second, the higher attention paid to perceived efficacy will result in a higher reduction in severity. For efficacy, both the cost and benefit are studied by the risk management team. That means the team will be able to understand better the nature and the consequences of the risk. With better understanding of the risk, it is logical to see that there will be a better reduction in severity as well.

Third, container terminal companies in Southeast Asian countries (not including Hong Kong and Mainland China) are less likely to have substantial reduction in risk severity compared to others. One possible reason could be the availability of insurance policies and regulations in those cities (such as Colombo) that facilitate the reduction of risk severity. Since the author does not have the information in hand to make a proper claim to this argument, further study on this particular subject is recommended.

Fourth, the reduction in severity is harder to implement in the Natural Disaster risk category than in the Social and Human risk category. The major difference between these two risk categories is whether the risk is caused by nature or caused by human beings. Obviously for those incidents that are artificial, it will be relatively easier for the management to handle and control, and therefore it is not unreasonable to come up with this result.

8.8 Conclusion

This book has provided some basic knowledge towards the operation of the terminal and the application of the SURE model in risk management of operation risk. Particularly, the application successfully demonstrated four import features of the SURE model. First, by modifying the elements from the well-known TPB model and the PADM model, this research has successfully developed a new risk management model – the SURE model for risk management in container terminal operations. This model is invented by the author and is the first of its kind in the risk management research field. This research has made use of this model for analysing the operational risk management of container terminals in Hong Kong, China and other Asian countries.

Second, through the questionnaire survey for the container terminals mentioned, the applicability of this model has been justified by analysing the qualitative part of this research, and so is the appropriateness of incorporating all eight risk attributes in the SURE model. The study also confirms the suitability of defining the six categories of risk in container terminal operations.

Third, the impacts of the attributes in the SURE model on risk responses under different risk categories are analysed. These relationships, together with the background and characteristics of the company being investigated, can help to reveal the common risk treatment practices for the industry. This is important as it turns the subjective risk assessment for terminal operations into an objective risk analysis.

Fourth, a few effective operational risk management strategies in container terminal operations have been identified, such as whether they should focus on probability reduction, severity reduction or both. In fact, terminal operators can also make use of the questionnaire in the study to reflect their stress and concerns over the risk elements so as to see how far their current methodologies and treatment practices deviate from the industry norm. Such action is reasonable, as, according to this study, most of the companies would observe and pay attention to the acts of other companies when tackling the risk events, especially when the risk events really occur. This can be reflected by the importance and significance of the subjective norm throughout the study.

However, when making reference to industry practice, the company should pay special attention to individual company characteristics in terms of background and business nature, as the effect of the risk treatment method will vary among companies possessing different characteristics.

More importantly, decision makers should go beyond traditional perception when handling risk events. For example, when targeting an effective way of reducing the severity of the risk events, focus should not be purely on severity itself. As demonstrated by this study, companies with such focus are unable to achieve high reduction in severity, whilst attention should be paid to the indirect aspects such as the efficacy of the risk responses.

Appendix 1
Questionnaire (Sample)

Thank you for your participation in this survey. The main purpose of this questionnaire is to identify the key attributes a container terminal will consider when determining the risk treatment method to the operational risks. This research, when completed, will help us in developing a new model in operational risk management.

This survey may take about 20~25 minutes to complete. If you have any queries in completing the questionnaire, please feel free to contact me at xxx-xxxxxxxx or xxx@xxx.com. Thanks again for your valuable time!

Part A: qualitative questions

In this questionnaire, we have identified 6 categories of operational risk for container terminals, they are:-

Table A1.1 Risk Category Classifications

Category	Descriptions
A	Natural Disaster (Typhoon, Tsunami, Earthquake, etc.)
B	Accident caused by External Event (ship colliding quay, terrorist)
C	Accident caused by Staff (carelessness, misconduct, etc.)
D	Breakdown/failure of Equipment (design fault, material fatigue, etc.)
E	Breakdown/failure of IT System (breakdown, hacker, etc.)
F	Social and Human Issue (labour strike, etc.)

Q1. Other than these 6 categories of risk, any other risk categories you consider important in the operational risk management of your company?

☐ No, these 6 categories have covered all.
☐ Yes, other risk categories include _____

Q2. Is there any standard procedure(s) in your company in selecting the risk treatment method for different categories of risk?

☐ No, we do not have any standard procedure.
☐ Yes, the procedure(s) include _____

Q3. In general, how long will it take for the management to make a decision on the risk treatment on a particular risk category?

☐ Within days   ☐ Within three months
☐ Within weeks   ☐ More than three months

Q4. Which party/parties will be involved in selecting the risk treatment method for operational risk of your company?

_____

_____

Q5. What are the limitation(s) that affect your company in selecting the most suitable risk treatment method?

_____

_____

Q6. How does your company measure the effectiveness of your risk treatment methods?

☐ No, we don't have any means to measure.
☐ Yes, our measurement method(s) is_____

_____

Q7. Do you communicate with external parties before you select the risk treatment method?

☐ No.
☐ Yes, we communicate with _____

Q8. Do you know what are the risk treatment methods adopted in the Industry?

☐ No.
☐ Yes some, but not all risk categories.
☐ Yes, I know what treatment methods are commonly adopted by the Industry.

Q9. Does the goals and objectives of your company affect your risk treatment methods decision?

☐ No.
☐ Yes some, but not for all risk categories.
☐ Yes, all risk treatment methods are in line with the goals and objectives of the company.

Q10. To what extent you consider the risk management strategy and/or the risk treatment methods affect your company image?

☐ No, not at all.
☐ Yes some, but not for all risk categories.
☐ Yes, the impact on company image will be considered in making all risk treatment method decisions.

Part B: quantitative questions

The risk before and after treatment will have its respective probability (P) and severity (S). The following table shows how the (P) and (S) are defined:

Probability (Chance of Occurrence)	P =	Severity (Monetary Loss, including both direct and indirect, in HKD)	S =
$P < 0.00001\%$	1	$S < 100$	1
$0.00001\% \leq P < 0.0001\%$	2	$100 \leq S < 1,000$	2
$0.0001\% \leq P < 0.001\%$	3	$1,000 \leq S < 10,000$	3
$0.001\% \leq P < 0.01\%$	4	$10,000 \leq S < 100,000$	4
$0.01\% \leq P < 0.1\%$	5	$100,000 \leq S < 1\ Mil$	5
$0.1\% \leq P < 1\%$	6	$1\ Mil \leq S < 10\ Mil$	6
$1\% \leq P < 10\%$	7	$10\ Mil \leq S < 100\ Mil$	7
$10\% \leq P < 100\%$	8	$100\ Mil \leq S$	8

For each of the risk category previously mentioned, please advise the respective probability and severity before and after the risk treatment method taken by your company.

Risk Category		Probability		Severity	
		Before	After	Before	After
A	Natural Disaster				
B	External Event				
C	Staff				
D	Equipment				
E	IT				
F	Social and Human				
G	[as in Q1]				
H	[as in Q1]				

In this survey, we assume there are eight attributes that affect your risk treatment method decision.

Evaluation Attributes	Description
Probability	The probability of a risk before risk treatment
Severity	The severity of a risk before risk treatment
Perceived Cost	Estimated cost (both direct and indirect) of the risk treatment method
Perceived Efficacy	Anticipated effectiveness of the risk treatment method

(Continued)

Goal and Objective	Business goal and objective of the company
Resource and Ability	How and how much an company can provide in dealing with a risk
Perceived Image	How the Customer feel about the way the company handle risk
Subjective Norm	The general practice the industry takes in dealing with a risk

For each risk category, the relative importance of these eight attributes will be different. In the following tables, we would like you to assess how important each attribute is when you deal with a particular risk category.

Risk Category (A) Natural Disaster	How Important this Attribute affect your selection of Risk Treatment Method?								
	Not Relevant						Very Important		
Evaluation Attributes	1	2	3	4	5	6	7	8	9
Probability	☐	☐	☐	☐	☐	☐	☐	☐	☐
Severity	☐	☐	☐	☐	☐	☐	☐	☐	☐
Perceived Cost	☐	☐	☐	☐	☐	☐	☐	☐	☐
Perceived Efficacy	☐	☐	☐	☐	☐	☐	☐	☐	☐
Goal and Objective	☐	☐	☐	☐	☐	☐	☐	☐	☐
Resource and Ability	☐	☐	☐	☐	☐	☐	☐	☐	☐
Perceived Image	☐	☐	☐	☐	☐	☐	☐	☐	☐
Subjective Norm	☐	☐	☐	☐	☐	☐	☐	☐	☐

Risk Category (B) External Events	How Important this Attribute affect your selection of Risk Treatment Method?								
	Not Relevant						Very Important		
Evaluation Attributes	1	2	3	4	5	6	7	8	9
Probability	☐	☐	☐	☐	☐	☐	☐	☐	☐
Severity	☐	☐	☐	☐	☐	☐	☐	☐	☐
Perceived Cost	☐	☐	☐	☐	☐	☐	☐	☐	☐
Perceived Efficacy	☐	☐	☐	☐	☐	☐	☐	☐	☐
Goal and Objective	☐	☐	☐	☐	☐	☐	☐	☐	☐
Resource and Ability	☐	☐	☐	☐	☐	☐	☐	☐	☐
Perceived Image	☐	☐	☐	☐	☐	☐	☐	☐	☐
Subjective Norm	☐	☐	☐	☐	☐	☐	☐	☐	☐

Risk Category (C) Staff's Acts	How Important this Attribute affect your selection of Risk Treatment Method?								
	Not Relevant						Very Important		
Evaluation Attributes	1	2	3	4	5	6	7	8	9
Probability	□	□	□	□	□	□	□	□	□
Severity	□	□	□	□	□	□	□	□	□
Perceived Cost	□	□	□	□	□	□	□	□	□
Perceived Efficacy	□	□	□	□	□	□	□	□	□
Goal and Objective	□	□	□	□	□	□	□	□	□
Resource and Ability	□	□	□	□	□	□	□	□	□
Perceived Image	□	□	□	□	□	□	□	□	□
Subjective Norm	□	□	□	□	□	□	□	□	□

Risk Category (D) Equipment	How Important this Attribute affect your selection of Risk Treatment Method?								
	Not Relevant						Very Important		
Evaluation Attributes	1	2	3	4	5	6	7	8	9
Probability	□	□	□	□	□	□	□	□	□
Severity	□	□	□	□	□	□	□	□	□
Perceived Cost	□	□	□	□	□	□	□	□	□
Perceived Efficacy	□	□	□	□	□	□	□	□	□
Goal and Objective	□	□	□	□	□	□	□	□	□
Resource and Ability	□	□	□	□	□	□	□	□	□
Perceived Image	□	□	□	□	□	□	□	□	□
Subjective Norm	□	□	□	□	□	□	□	□	□

Risk Category (E) System	How Important this Attribute affect your selection of Risk Treatment Method?								
	Not Relevant						Very Important		
Evaluation Attributes	1	2	3	4	5	6	7	8	9
Probability	□	□	□	□	□	□	□	□	□
Severity	□	□	□	□	□	□	□	□	□
Perceived Cost	□	□	□	□	□	□	□	□	□
Perceived Efficacy	□	□	□	□	□	□	□	□	□

Goal and Objective	☐	☐	☐	☐	☐	☐	☐	☐	☐
Resource and Ability	☐	☐	☐	☐	☐	☐	☐	☐	☐
Perceived Image	☐	☐	☐	☐	☐	☐	☐	☐	☐
Subjective Norm	☐	☐	☐	☐	☐	☐	☐	☐	☐

Risk Category *(F) Social Issues*	*How Important this Attribute affect your selection of Risk Treatment Method?*								
	Not Relevant						*Very Important*		
Evaluation Attributes	*1*	*2*	*3*	*4*	*5*	*6*	*7*	*8*	*9*
Probability	☐	☐	☐	☐	☐	☐	☐	☐	☐
Severity	☐	☐	☐	☐	☐	☐	☐	☐	☐
Perceived Cost	☐	☐	☐	☐	☐	☐	☐	☐	☐
Perceived Efficacy	☐	☐	☐	☐	☐	☐	☐	☐	☐
Goal and Objective	☐	☐	☐	☐	☐	☐	☐	☐	☐
Resource and Ability	☐	☐	☐	☐	☐	☐	☐	☐	☐
Perceived Image	☐	☐	☐	☐	☐	☐	☐	☐	☐
Subjective Norm	☐	☐	☐	☐	☐	☐	☐	☐	☐

Risk Category *(G) [as in Q1]*	*How Important this Attribute affect your selection of Risk Treatment Method?*								
	Not Relevant						*Very Important*		
Evaluation Attributes	*1*	*2*	*3*	*4*	*5*	*6*	*7*	*8*	*9*
Probability	☐	☐	☐	☐	☐	☐	☐	☐	☐
Severity	☐	☐	☐	☐	☐	☐	☐	☐	☐
Perceived Cost	☐	☐	☐	☐	☐	☐	☐	☐	☐
Perceived Efficacy	☐	☐	☐	☐	☐	☐	☐	☐	☐
Goal and Objective	☐	☐	☐	☐	☐	☐	☐	☐	☐
Resource and Ability	☐	☐	☐	☐	☐	☐	☐	☐	☐
Perceived Image	☐	☐	☐	☐	☐	☐	☐	☐	☐
Subjective Norm	☐	☐	☐	☐	☐	☐	☐	☐	☐

Risk Category *(H) [as in Q1]*	*How Important this Attribute affect your selection of Risk Treatment Method?*								
	Not Relevant						*Very Important*		
Evaluation Attributes	*1*	*2*	*3*	*4*	*5*	*6*	*7*	*8*	*9*
Probability	☐	☐	☐	☐	☐	☐	☐	☐	☐

Severity	☐	☐	☐	☐	☐	☐	☐	☐	☐
Perceived Cost	☐	☐	☐	☐	☐	☐	☐	☐	☐
Perceived Efficacy	☐	☐	☐	☐	☐	☐	☐	☐	☐
Goal and Objective	☐	☐	☐	☐	☐	☐	☐	☐	☐
Resource and Ability	☐	☐	☐	☐	☐	☐	☐	☐	☐
Perceived Image	☐	☐	☐	☐	☐	☐	☐	☐	☐
Subjective Norm	☐	☐	☐	☐	☐	☐	☐	☐	☐

Part C: demographic analysis

Description			*Explanation*
Location	HK/Macau	☐	Hong Kong and Macau SAR only
	Southern China	☐	Guangdong, Guangxi, Fujian and along Pearl River
	Eastern China	☐	Shanghai, Zhejiang, Jiangsu and along Yangtze River
	Northern China	☐	Shandong, Tianjin, Liaoning and around Bohai Area
Customer Base	Domestic	☐	> 50% container throughput in domestic trade
	International	☐	> 50% container throughput in international trade
Shareholding	State-Owned	☐	Company dominantly owned by the state-owned enterprise
	Joint Venture	☐	Company dominantly owned by foreign investor
	Private Entity	☐	Company dominantly owned by local private company
Management	Full International	☐	3 or more senior managements are expatriates (incl. HK)
	Semi-international	☐	1 to 2 senior managements are expatriates (incl. HK)
	Local	☐	All senior management are locals
Terminal Size	> 70,000 DWT	☐	Capable of berthing 70,000 DWT or above vessel
	10 ~ 70K DWT	☐	Capable of berthing 10,000 to 70,000 DWT vessel
	< 10,000 DWT	☐	Capable of berthing < 10,000 DWT vessel only

Personal details (optional)

Company Name:					
Respondent Name:					
Respondent Position:					
Years of Experience in CT Operations:	☐ Below 10	☐ 10~15	☐ 15~20	☐ 20~25	☐ Above 25
Respondent Age Group:	☐ Below 30	☐ 30~40	☐ 40~50	☐ 50~60	☐ Above 60
Respondent Gender:	☐ Male	☐ Female			

Internal use:

Reference No.		Date Received:	
Analysis by:		Date Analysed:	

References

Ajzen, I. (1991). The theory of planned behavior. *Organizational Behavior and Human Decision Processes, 50,* 179–211.

Al-Bahar, J. F., & Crandall, K. C. (1990). Systematic risk management approach for construction projects. *Journal of Construction Engineering and Management, 116*(3), 533–546.

Aven, T. (2012). Foundational issues in risk assessment and risk management. *Risk Analysis, 32*(10), 1647–1656.

Bernstein, P. L. (1996). *Against the gods: The remarkable story of risk.* New York, NY: John Wiley & Sons.

Boodman, D. M. (1987). Managing business risk. *Interfaces, 17*(2), 91–96.

Bubeck, P., Botzen, W.J.W., & Aerts, J.C.J.H. (2012). A review of risk perceptions and other factors that influence flood mitigation behaviour. *Risk Analysis, 32*(9), 1481–1495.

Code of Practice for the Design of Seaport Container Terminals, P. R. China, (JTS165–4–2011), Ministry of Communications.

Cole, F. L. (1988). Content analysis: Process and application. *Clinical Nurse Specialist, 2*(1), 53–57.

COSO (Committee of Sponsoring Organizations of the Treadway Commission). (2004). *COSO Enterprise Risk Management – Integrated Framework: Executive Summary.*

Cullinane, K., Wang, T.F., Song, D.W., & Ji, P. (2006). The technical efficiency of container ports: Comparing data envelopment analysis and stochastic frontier analysis. *Transportation Research Part A: Policy and Practice, 40*(4), 354–374.

Davies, J., Finlay, M., McLenaghen, T., & Wilson, D. (2006). Key risk indicators – their role in operational risk management and measurement. *ARM and Risk Business International*, Prague, 1–32.

Eagly, A. H., & Chaiken, S. (1993). *The psychology of attitudes.* Orlando, FL: Harcourt Brace Jovanovich College Publishers.

Elo, S., & Kyngas, H. (2007).The qualitative content analysis process. *Journal of Advanced Nursing, 62*(1), 107–115.

Eloff, E., Labuschagne, L., & Badenhorst, B. (1993). A comparative framework for risk analysis methods. *Computers & Security, 12*(6), 597–603.

Fischhoff, B., Watson, S.R., & Hope, C. (1984). Defining risk. *Policy Sciences, 17*(2), 123–139.

Greene, W. H., (1993). *Econometric analysis.* New York, NY: Macmillan

Griffin, R. J., Dunwoody, S., & Neuwirth, K. (1999). Proposed model of the relationship of risk information seeking and processing to the development of preventive behaviours. *Environmental Research, 80*(2), S230–S245.

Haimes, Y. Y., Lambert, J. H., & Kaplan, S. (2002). Risk filtering, ranking, and management framework using hierarchical holographic modelling. *Risk Analysis, 22*(2), 383–397.

Hale, J. L., Householder, B. J. & Greene, K. L. (2003). *The theory of reasoned action. In J. P. Dillard & M. Pfau (Eds.), The persuasion handbook: Developments in theory and practice* (pp. 259–286). Thousand Oaks, CA: Sage.

Harwood, T. G., & Garry, T. (2003). An overview of content analysis. *The Marketing Review, 3,* 479–498.

Heinrich, H. W. (1931). *Industrial accident prevention: A scientific approach.* New York, NY: McGraw-Hill.

Herzberg, F. I. (1966). *Work and the nature of man.* Oxford, UK: Oxford, World.

Hoffman, D. L., & Batra, R. (1991). Viewer response to programs: Dimensionality and concurrent behavior. *Journal of Advertising Research,* August/September, 46–56.

Hoffman, D. L., & Leeuw, J. D. (1992). Interpreting multiple correspondence analysis as a multidimensional scaling method. *Marketing Letters, 3*(3), 259–272.

Holsti, Ole R. (1969). *Content analysis for the social sciences and humanities.* Reading, MA: Addison-Wesley.

Hubbard, D. W. (2009). *The failure of risk management: Why it's broken and how to fix it.* Hoboken, NJ: Wiley.

The Institute of Operational Risk. (2010). *Operational risk sound practice guidance – operational risk governance,* Sep. 2010. www.ior-institute.org/public/RiskGovernanceFinal.pdf

Kaplan, S., & Garrick, B. J. (1981). On the quantitative definition of risk. *Risk Analysis, 1*(1), 11–27.

Khan, O., & Burnes, B. (2007). Risk and supply chain management: creating a research agenda. *International Journal of Logistics Management,* 18(2), 197–216.

Leung, F., Santos, R., & Haimes, Y. (2003). Risk modelling, assessment, and management of lahar flow threat. *Risk Analysis, 23*(6), 1323–1335.

Levinson, Marc (2006). *The box: How the shipping container made the world smaller and the world economy bigger.* Princeton, NJ: Princeton University Press.

Lewis, M. A. (2003). Cause, consequence and control: Towards a theoretical and practical model of operational risk. *Journal of Operations Management, 21*(2), 205–224.

Li, K. X., & Cullinane, K. (2003). An economic approach to maritime risk management and safety regulation. *Maritime Economics & Logistics, 5*(3), 268–284.

Lindell, M. K., & Perry, R. W. (2012). The protective action decision model: Theoretical modifications and additional evidence. *Risk Analysis, 32*(4), 616–632.

Madden, T. J., Ellen, P. S., & Ajzen, I. (1992). A comparison of the theory of planned behaviour and the theory of reasoned action. *Personality and Social Psychology Bulletin, 18*(1), 3–9.

March, J. G., & Shapira, Z. (1987). Managerial perspectives on risk and risk taking. *Management Science, 33*(11), 1404–1418.

Mathieson, K. (1991). Predicting user intentions: Comparing the technology acceptance model with the theory of planned behaviour. *Information Systems Research, 2*(3), 173–191.

Mayo, A. J., & Nohria, N. (2005, October 3). Harvard business school weekly. *The Truck Driver Who Reinvented Shipping.* http://hbswk.hbs.edu/item/5026.html

Morgan, M. G., Florig, H. K., deKay, M. L., & Fischbeck, P. (2000). Categorizing risks for risk ranking. *Risk Analysis: An International Journal, 20*(1), 49–58.

Morris, M. G., Venkatesh, V., & Ackerman, P. L. (2005). Gender and age differences in employee decisions about new technology: An extension to the theory of planned behavior. *Engineering Management, IEEE Transactions, 52*(1), 69–84.

Mosteller, F., (1948). A k-sample slippage test for an extreme population. *The Annals of Mathematical Statistics, 19*(1), 58–65.

Nationalbank, O., & Finanzmarkt, A.A.D. (2006). *Guidelines on operational risk management. OeNB and FMA.* Oesterreichische Nationalbank and Austrian Financial Market Authority. Vienna, Austria. www.fma.gv.at/typo3conf/ext/dam_download/secure.php?u=0&file=2142&t=1422313906&hash=07e9f5446cec43e4a6f116008fd18d56

Norrman, A., & Lindroth, R. (2004). Categorization of supply chain risk and risk management. In C. Brindley (Ed.), *Supply chain risk.* Ashgate, UK: Aldershot.

Paté-Cornell, E. (2012). On 'black swans' and 'perfect storms': Risk analysis and management when statistics are not enough. *Risk Analysis, 32*(11), 1823–1833.

Rao, S., & Goldsby, T. J. (2009). Supply chain risks: A review and typology. *International Journal of Logistics Management, 20*(1), 97–123.

Roe, Anne. (1953). *The making of a scientist.* New York, NY: Dodd, Mead & Co.

Shang, K. C., & Tseng, W. J. (2010). A risk analysis of stevedoring operations in seaport container terminals. *Journal of Marine Science and Technology, 18*(2), 201–210.

Siegrist, M., & Gutscher, H. (2008). Natural hazards and motivation for mitigation behavior: People cannot predict the affect evoked by a severe flood. *Risk Analysis, 28*(3), 771–778.

Steenken, D., Voß, S., & Stahlbock, R. (2004). Container terminal operation and operations research – a classification and literature review. *OR Spectrum, 26*(1), 3–49.

Sung, M. J. (2005). *The modern risk management.* Taipei: Wu-Nan Book Inc.

Tummala, V.M.R., & Mak, C. L. (2001). A risk management model for improving operation and maintenance activities in electricity transmission networks. *The Journal of the Operational Research Society, 52*(2), 125–134.

Vis, I. F., & De Koster, R. (2003). Transshipment of containers at a container terminal: An overview. *European Journal of Operational Research, 147*(1), 1–16.

Ward, S. (2003). Approaches to integrated risk management: A multi-dimensional framework. *Risk Management, 5*(4), 7–23.

Whitfield, R. N. (2003). *Managing institutional risks – a framework.* A Dissertation in Higher Education Management for the Degree of Doctor of Education, University of Pennsylvania.

Wu, J. H. (2011). *Risk assessment model on evaluating ERP projects case study.* Thesis, College of Business Administration, Hunan University, China.

Yin, R. K. (2009). *Case study research: Design and methods.* Los Angeles, CA: Sage Publications.

Index

twenty-feet equivalent unit (TEU), defined 2
Type III error (Mosteller) 48–9

ultra-large container vessel (ULCV) 6–7
uniplanar, use of term 65
United States: container ports, ranked 8, *72–3*; history of containerization in 1, 4; Jacksonville, Florida terminal accident (2008) 41; survey on cost of risk against revenue 46

vessel operation system (VOS) 29

Ward, S. 51
Whitfield, R. N. 64
World International Organization for Standardization (ISO) 4
World Shipping Council 40
Wu, J. H. 43

yard operation system (YOS) 29 *see also* container terminal operations